TEST YOUR DRIVING IQ

Susan McCormack &
Tina Janson-Caddel

**Published by BSM in association with
Virgin Publishing**

We won't fail you

First published in Great Britain in 2001 by
Virgin Publishing Ltd
Thames Wharf Studios
Rainville Road
London W6 9HA

ISBN 0 7535 0549 5

Designed and typeset by Eric Drewery
Printed and bound in Great Britain by Mackays of Chatham, Kent

CONTENTS

INTRODUCTION

Welcome to *Test Your Driving IQ*. Designed to be fun and entertaining with a serious edge, *Test Your Driving IQ* assesses your knowledge of driving.

The book is divided into four sections.

The first three sections form the main body of *Test Your Driving IQ*. Each section contains five tests of 40 questions.

Generally speaking, the questions in the first section are easier than those in the second section, which, in turn, are easier than those in the third section. The questions are easier in the sense that they may be asking for straightforward information and the answers may just contain one word, whereas Section Three questions may be looking for an in-depth understanding of driving-related issues and the answers needed may contain several words.

For example, a question from Section One is: What is the national speed limit for cars and motorcycles on a dual carriageway?

With a question like this you either know the answer is 70 mph or you don't.

A question from Section Three might read: Two of the most common failure points in the practical driving test for car drivers are 'not making effective use of the mirrors well before changing direction' and 'incorrect use of the controls when reversing'.

Which one is the more common reason for failure? You may not know the answer to this question, however you may well be able to make a sensible guess that an 'incorrect use of the controls when reversing' is a more common reason for failure than 'not making effective use of the mirrors'.

At the end of Section Three you can find all the answers and explanations to the questions in the previous 15 tests. These tell you how to score yourself. Every question carries one point, unless specifically indicated otherwise. For example, there is more than one part to certain of the questions and these carry one point for each part correctly answered. You can use the space provided to fill in your answers and note down your final score for each test.

The questions in these 15 tests cover all manner of driving-related issues, from how to drive manual and automatic cars, to large goods vehicles, coaches and motorcycles, to separation distances, route knowledge, traffic signs, mechanics, environmental issues, and dealing with different road and weather conditions.

The core theme is driver safety. It is generally accepted that most accidents are caused by driver error. In many cases the attitude of the driver contributes to the error being made. Imagine a driver has committed an error, resulting in an accident, for example by driving too fast for the conditions, and that this is a result not of improper use of the accelerator but of a mistaken or deliberate misuse of speed. The reason for this mistaken or deliberate misuse of speed is related to the attitude and the value system of the driver. In other words the driver does not consider that respecting speed limits, whether imposed by law or necessitated by conditions, is important.

Furthermore, knowledge impinges on attitude – what we know affects how we drive. Consider a question like the one above from Section One: What is the national speed limit for cars and motorcycles on a dual carriageway?

If you don't know that the national speed limit is 60 mph on a single carriageway and 70 mph on a dual carriageway, then you may mistakenly err in your choice of a safe speed for the road and your error could lead to an accident.

Test Your Driving IQ helps keep you safer as a driver because it tests your knowledge and fills in any gaps.

Test 16 is the IQ test. You collate this yourself based on the answers you gave to specific questions from the previous 15 tests and you are guided through the steps you need to take to come up with your driving IQ score. You can then compare your score against the sample and read what your score indicates in relation to your driver knowledge. You can read how the IQ test was designed and validated, based on a sample of 2,760 people answering these IQ questions, and see a range of statistics based on data collected.

The fourth section consists of three fun tests of 40 questions, aimed at testing your trivia motoring knowledge and covering aspects from BSM and instructor training, to songs with driving themes, to celebrities and their motorcars, to car manufacturers.

The answers to these three tests are at the end of Section Four.

What is the best way to drive? This is not a straightforward question to answer. Some people may feel that 'best' means 'most skilful'; where others may interpret 'best' as 'safest'. *Test Your Driving IQ* considers 'best' to mean 'safest'. The questions therefore are based on the *Highway Code* and the Driving Standards Agency's *Driving Manual*. The answers will always be the ones that conform to the guidance given in these publications. If you would like to take issue with any of the questions or answers then you can visit the BSM website at www.bsm.co.uk and email us with your comments.

Finally, please enjoy *Test Your Driving IQ*. You can choose to work your way through every test, completing all the questions and finishing up with your own IQ score. Alternatively, you may wish to dip into the tests and answer questions here and there. You could turn straight to the IQ test and complete it by referring back to the specified questions in the other 15 tests. Or, again, you might want to head straight for Section Four and test your trivia driving knowledge with the fun tests. Whichever way you choose to use this book, our aim is that you enjoy answering the questions and take away from it some useful hints and tips on safe driving.

SECTION ONE
TEST 1

1 Before driving you must ensure that your seating position

   a is a comfortable one

   b is close to the controls

   c allows you to reach and use the controls easily

   d allows you to operate the controls by stretching

2 Look at Fig. 1 on Plate A and identify which *Highway Code* rule, regarding being seen, the leading rider is following that the rider behind is not.

_____

3 What is the minimum legal age to hold a provisional moped licence?

_____

4 Traffic crashes account for what proportion of all accidental deaths in Britain?

_____

5 Identify the sign Fig. 2 on Plate A.

_____

6 You are about to take the next road on the left. As you look into the road and start to steer, you notice pedestrians are just starting to cross the road. Would you

   a blast the horn to warn them you are there?

   b give way to them?

   c accelerate to get past them sooner?

7 What is the most common driver error that causes crashes?

_____

8 You are on a dry road surface in good condition. Your vehicle has good brakes and tyres. What is the shortest overall stopping distance at 40 mph?

_____

9 When the rear of a vehicle is skidding to the left as a result of an attempt at an emergency stop, the best way for the driver to regain control is by

   a cadence braking, steering to the left and then right

   b pumping the brake, steering to the right and then left

   c keeping the brake applied and steering out of the skid

   d keeping the brake applied and selecting neutral

10 If you have a full car licence, what type of motorcycle can you ride after completing a CBT course?

_____

11 What is the national speed limit for cars and motorcycles on a dual carriageway?

_____

12 How can you check that the wheels are running 'true' on a motorcycle?

_____

13 The routine MSPSL is used to approach junctions. What do the letters MSPSL stand for?

_____

14 As you approach a junction on the left where you intend turning, there is a cyclist just in front of you. Would you

   a accelerate to get past the cyclist so that you can make the turn? ☐

   b blast the horn to warn the cyclist you are there? ☐

   c slow down and hang back until the cyclist has cleared the junction? ☐

15 Look at Fig. 3 on Plate A. Obviously you need to be aware that cattle may be crossing the road at milking time. Of what else should you also be aware when you see this sign, in relation to the road?

_____

16 Name the voluntary organisation set up on the initiative of the Government to enable disabled people to use their mobility benefit to obtain a car.

_____

17 When travelling down a steep hill in a vehicle fitted with automatic transmission the driver should

   a brake whilst going down the hill, leaving the mechanism to lock up automatically ☐

   b brake as necessary on the approach and select a lower gear before descending ☐

   c select a lower gear and then brake during the descent ☐

   d select 'sports mode' programme where this is fitted ☐

18 For how long may blue badge holders park on single or double yellow lines in England and Wales?

_____

19 You are driving a vehicle not fitted with anti-lock brakes. How can 'wheel lock' be controlled during heavy braking?

   a By using engine braking ☐

   b By cadence braking ☐

   c By braking suddenly ☐

   d By using clutch and brake together ☐

20 You can only tow a trailer with your motorcycle on three conditions. Can you name them?

_____

_____

_____

21 You are approaching a level crossing with lights controlling the traffic. If a train is approaching what sequence of lights will you see?

a An amber light followed by twin flashing red lights.

b An amber light followed by a red light.

c A flashing amber light followed by twin steady red lights.

22 Name four emergency vehicles with blue flashing lights.

_____ _____

_____

23 Imagine you are the driver of a large vehicle. The Vehicle Inspectorate, which is carrying out spot checks on large vehicles, has delayed your journey. Your vehicle has been noted as having a major defect. Who will be notified of this defect?

_____

24 Is it compulsory to carry a first aid kit in your car in Austria?

_____

25 What does Fig. 4 on Plate A mean?

_____

26 You have just purchased a new vehicle with ABS fitted. What does ABS mean?

_____

27 A main consideration when driving defensively is to

   a keep just within the speed limit at all times ☐
   b always give way to other drivers, showing courtesy and consideration ☐
   c drive slowly and cautiously ☐
   d drive at a speed that suits the road and traffic conditions ☐

28 What is the blood alcohol legal limit at which you may drive a car in Austria?

_____

29 You are driving a Passenger Carrying Vehicle (PCV) over 7.5 tonne and with more than eight seats. Are you allowed to drive in the third lane of a motorway?

_____

30 A driver's thinking distance is based on the period of travel from

   a noticing the hazard to the point when braking begins ☐
   b noticing the hazard until when the vehicle stops ☐
   c the point when the brakes are first applied until when the car stops ☐
   d the point after two seconds have been counted ☐

31 In Switzerland motorcyclists must not overtake a column of vehicles or weave between vehicles. True or false?

_____

32 Look at Fig. 5 on Plate A and imagine you are approaching this junction with the intention of turning left. What action would you take first?

_____

33 The law states that side reflectors must be fitted to trailers longer than what distance?

_____

34 You are about to overtake a motorcyclist. The rider looks over the right shoulder. It is most likely that

  a the rider intends moving to the right
  b something has fallen from the machine
  c the rear tyre is flat
  d it would be safe and correct to overtake

35 What is an International Motor Insurance Certificate more commonly known as?

_____

36 What is known as the 'wave effect' when driving Large Goods Tankers?

_____

_____

37 What three things should you urgently check where a casualty is unconscious at a road crash?

_____

_____

_____

38 When travelling along a one-way street towards a crossroads where a white triangle is painted on the road, the

   a single broken white lines will run across the whole width of the road ☐

   b single broken white lines will run across half the width of the road ☐

   c double broken white lines will run across half the width of the road ☐

   d double broken white lines will run across the whole width of the road ☐

39 Large Goods Vehicles (LGV) driving along a three-lane motorway

   a are allowed to use all three lanes ☐

   b are allowed to use the left-hand lane only unless directed otherwise by road signs or traffic controllers ☐

   c are allowed to use the left and centre lanes only unless directed otherwise by road signs or traffic controllers ☐

   d can only use the hard shoulder unless directed otherwise by road signs or traffic controllers ☐

40 Whom must you notify when, as a vehicle owner, you buy or sell your vehicle, or change your name or address?

Total score for Test 1 _____

SECTION ONE
TEST 2

1 A vehicle will have the most stability when its driver is

   a accelerating gently when travelling in a straight line

   b reducing speed by decelerating

   c applying normal pressure to the footbrake

   d applying firm pressure to the footbrake

2 Look at Fig. 1 on Plate B and identify two risk areas that the cyclist should be particularly aware of when cycling along this type of road with parked cars.

_____

_____

3 You are riding a motorcycle and sidecar outfit with single wheel drive (rear wheel of motorcycle). When you accelerate, what is the outfit likely to do?

_____

_____

4 What is the shortest stopping distance at 30 mph in metres?

_____

5 Look at Fig. 2 on Plate B. What does this sign mean?

_____

6 Which vehicle is most likely to be affected by crosswinds?

  a Lorry.

  b Car.

  c Motorcycle.

7 What is the overall stopping distance made up of?

_____

8 What is the name given to the European arrangement of on-street parking concessions for severely disabled people?

_____

9 You are driving a vehicle on a motorway. A front tyre bursts. You should

  a loosen your grip on the steering wheel

  b brake firmly to a stop

  c hold the steering wheel firmly

  d select neutral

10 Motorcycles used after 1 January 1985 must have what marked, certifying it is of an approved type?

_____

11 Is a disabled person in receipt of the higher rate of mobility component of the Disabled Living Allowance exempt from Vehicle Excise Duty?

_____

12 Cyclists are allowed on motorways as long as they stay within the boundaries of the hard shoulder. True or false?

_____

13 Name the emergency vehicle that uses a green flashing light.

_____

14 Why should you keep your speed right down when driving on roads where there are lots of parked cars?

a Because the speed limit is 20 mph. ☐
b Because children might run out between the parked cars. ☐
c Because the stopping distance will be longer. ☐

15 Look at Fig. 3 on Plate B and imagine that you are driving on a country road when you see this sign. Should you be more careful approaching a left-hand bend or a right-hand bend?

_____

16 Motorists driving abroad in Spain, who wear glasses for driving, must ensure that a spare pair is carried in the vehicle. True or false?

_____

17 Look at Fig. 4 on Plate B and imagine you are approaching this hazard. There is a warning sign on the opposite side of the ford. What will the warning sign tell you to do?

_____

18 When you or your family are taken ill or require treatment when you are abroad in European Economic Area Countries, what is the name of the form you must produce?

_____

19 The driver of a car fitted with automatic transmission should select a lower gear before

   a descending a hill

   b travelling up a hill

   c travelling round a corner

   d stopping suddenly

20 Imagine you are driving in Italy. You intend taking the first exit at the roundabout ahead. How and when would you signal your intentions to other road users?

_____

_____

21 The main function of Anti-lock Braking Systems (ABS) is to

   a allow the vehicle to stop in a shorter distance

   b make sure the wheels lock up fully

   c aid steering while braking

22 Who is responsible for ensuring that children under the age of 14 wear seat belts or sit in an approved child restraint?

_____

23 Of what three things should a driver of a double decker bus be aware when driving along roads with a steep camber, with particular reference to the camber?

_____

_____

_____

24 To whom must you report any health condition likely to affect your driving?

_____

25 Look at Fig. 5 on Plate B. If you were driving in the right-hand lane, what would the sign be telling you to do?

_____

26 Learner car drivers are allowed on the motorway to practise as long as they are with a qualified driving instructor. True or false?

_____

27 When a vehicle's power-assisted steering mechanism fails

   a the steering will lock up completely

   b this will cause more wear on the tyres

   c the steering will feel heavier

   d the steering will feel lighter

28 What is the speed limit on a road with street lights and no signs showing a speed limit?

_____

29 When driving in snowy conditions, the *Highway Code* advises you to carry four things with you in case of an emergency. What are they?

_____

_____

_____

_____

30 Where there is a line of parked cars well ahead on the left it is
   a unnecessary to signal
   b not always necessary to signal
   c necessary to signal if other traffic is following
   d incorrect to signal

31 What colour reflective road studs mark the lanes or the middle of the road?

_____

32 Look at Fig. 6 on Plate B and decide whether, as a driver, you should treat this as one or two crossings?

_____

33 Which lane on a motorway can you not enter unless directed by road signs or traffic controllers when driving a large goods vehicle?

_____

34 On a two-way road with three lanes, a driver already in the middle lane has

  a priority over oncoming traffic in the same lane ☐

  b no more priority than oncoming traffic in the same lane ☐

  c more priority than oncoming traffic that hasn't yet moved into the middle lane ☐

  d less priority than oncoming traffic that hasn't yet moved into the middle lane ☐

35 Can trams steer to avoid you?

_____

36 Imagine you are driving a Large Goods Vehicle. The time now is 12 noon. You have been driving since 8 am. Under EU rules, how much longer can you continue without a break?

_____

37 In icy or snowy weather how much greater can stopping distances be than on dry roads?

_____

38 When joining a motorway from an acceleration lane a driver's speed should be

a slightly slower than the traffic in the left-hand lane ☐

b the same as the traffic in the left-hand lane ☐

c slightly faster than the traffic in the left-hand lane ☐

d much faster than the traffic in the left-hand lane ☐

39 How long must defect reports from drivers of large vehicles be kept, by law?

_____

40 When parking your vehicle for a short time, is it illegal to leave it with the engine running?

_____

Total score for Test 2 _____

47

SECTION ONE
TEST 3

1 When braking which tyres have the most grip on the road?

  a The front tyres

  b The rear tyres

  c All four tyres have equal grip

2 Look at Fig. 1 on Plate C. The photo shows a white van and a red car in the left-hand lane, both travelling at the 40 mph speed limit. What is the safety rule the red car is breaking?

_____

3 What is the minimum driving licence requirement to drive unaccompanied in a three-wheeled vehicle, such as a Reliant Robin?

_____

4 What are you required to display on the back of any UK registered motor vehicle, caravan or trailer that you use on roads abroad, that you do not have to display in the UK?

_____

5 Fig. 2 on Plate C shows a police officer controlling traffic at a major junction. You are approaching the front of the queue of traffic. What signal is the officer giving you?

_____

6 The driver must ensure that all children under what age wear seat belts or sit in an approved child restraint?

  a 14 years.
  b 15 years.
  c 16 years.

7 If you park your car at night in a lay-by on a road where the speed limit is 40 mph, must you leave any lights switched on?

_____

8 What does it mean if you see red lights flash on a signal in the central reservation of a motorway?

_____

9 After a long dry spell of weather, roads will be more slippery after it has

  a just started to rain
  b been raining for a long time
  c stopped raining heavily
  d stopped raining completely

10 You are riding your motorcycle along a two-lane motorway. Which lane are you advised to use for normal riding?

_____

11 What shape are signs giving instructions to tram drivers?

_____

12 You're driving a Passenger Carrying Vehicle (PCV) and you break down on the motorway. You have several passengers on board. What is the very first thing you should do once you've stopped on the hard shoulder?

_____

13 What is road tax more formally known as?

_____

14 The _Highway Code_ indicates that

a it is best to avoid the use of any type of telephone while driving ☐

b it is safe to use a mobile phone while driving if it can be used hands free ☐

c there is no difference between hands-free and hand-held telephones ☐

15 Look at Fig. 3 on Plate C. What should you do after driving through this situation and why?

_____

_____

_____

16 From what age does a vehicle require a current M.O.T. test certificate?

_____

17 Look at Fig. 4 on Plate C. Is this driver doing anything wrong?

_____

_____

18 If a police officer asks to see your driving documents and you do not have them with you, within how many days must you produce them at a police station?

_____

19 On a vehicle fitted with automatic transmission you would use 'kickdown' to

- **a** give quicker acceleration
- **b** stop in an emergency
- **c** pull up smoothly
- **d** go down a steep hill

20 The *Highway Code* recommends that drivers should have a break after every

- **a** one hour of driving
- **b** two hours of driving
- **c** three hours of driving

21 What is a toucan crossing?

_____

22 What is the legal minimum insurance cover you must have to drive on public roads?

_____

23 By law everyone must wear a safety helmet when riding a motorcycle on the road. True or false?

_____

24 If your car needs an M.O.T. certificate and you drive without one, what could be invalidated?

_____

25 Look at Fig. 5 on Plate C. Where would you see this sign and what should you do when you see it?

_____

26 In Europe, most 17-year-olds are not allowed to drive a motorcar. True or false?

_____

27 Where there are double white lines painted in the centre of the road and the line nearest the driver is broken, a driver may

   a cross or straddle the lines to overtake when safe to do so
   b not cross or straddle the lines
   c park on the left
   d park, subject to restrictions

28 What is the legal minimum depth of tread for cars, light vans and light trailers?

_____

29 You are approaching road works and have just passed a temporary maximum speed limit of 40 mph. Must you adhere to this speed limit?

a Yes, you must not exceed any temporary speed restriction. ☐

b Yes; however, you can exceed the temporary speed restriction if there is no other traffic along the same stretch of road. ☐

c No, temporary speed restrictions only apply in adverse weather conditions. ☐

30 A driver pulls out of a side road in front of you causing you to brake hard. You should

a ignore the error and stay calm ☐

b flash your lights to display your annoyance ☐

c sound your horn to display your annoyance ☐

d overtake as soon as possible ☐

31 What term is used to describe the fact that the piston is at the bottom of its stroke in its cycle?

_____

32 Look at Fig. 6 on Plate C. If you saw this sign what road would you be on?

_____

33 When can you overtake on the left on the motorway?

_____

34 When turning right from a road which is only just wide enough for one line of traffic each way, a driver will need to position the vehicle

  a well over to the left

  b just left of the road centre

  c in the middle of the road

  d well back from the 'Give Way' lines

35 Name the device used to measure the rotary speed of an engine, shaft, gear, etc. in rotations (revolutions) per minute.

_____

36 What does a yellow and red stripe on the back of a Large Goods Vehicle mean?

_____

_____

37 Leaded petrol has not been available anywhere in the EC since January 2000. A substitute is sold at the pumps. Name this substitute.

_____

38 You are driving at the maximum speed limit on a clear motorway. You should keep to

  a any one of the lanes

  b the middle lane

  c the right-hand lane

  d the left-hand lane

39 If you were towing a caravan and about to overtake a horse, which two important issues should you be aware of? The road ahead is clear and it is safe to overtake.

_____

_____

40 Name the device used to cut down the amount of harmful exhaust gases released into the atmosphere through the car's exhaust.

_____

Total score for Test 3 _____

42

SECTION ONE
TEST 4

1 The distance in which a vehicle can be brought
to a sudden stop depends mainly on the

   a driver's eyesight

   b speed the vehicle is travelling at

   c braking efficiency

   d gear selected

2 Look at Fig. 1 on Plate D. As a driver what
would cause you some concern if you were
driving along this road?

_____

3 Cyclists can use bus lanes at all times. True or
false?

_____

4 If you do not have a current M.O.T. test
certificate for your vehicle what will you not be
able to renew?

_____

5 Identify sign Fig. 2 on Plate D.

_____

6 What might it mean if a motorcyclist checks over his right shoulder whilst you are following?

   a The motorcyclist could soon attempt to turn right. ☐

   b The motorcyclist has perhaps dropped something. ☐

   c The motorcyclist is not sure where he wants to go. ☐

7 For how long is an M.O.T. certificate normally valid?

_____

8 What is the legal minimum depth of tyre tread for motorcycles, large vehicles and passenger carrying vehicles?

_____

9 When driving through deep water you should drive

   a slowly in a low gear with engine speed high ☐

   b slowly in a high gear with engine speed low ☐

   c quickly in an intermediate gear ☐

   d at a normal speed in a high gear ☐

10 You are riding your motorcycle along a normal road at 40 mph. The conditions are dry and good. What is the minimum stopping distance?

_____

11 Name the steel canister, fitted to some vehicles, containing a ceramic honeycomb material coated with a substance which speeds up a chemical change without being altered itself.

_____

12 You are leaving your motorcycle and sidecar outfit parked outside on a slight uphill gradient. Which two measures should you take to ensure it doesn't roll away?

_____

_____

13 Name the gas that gives off a strong 'rotten egg' smell when a car fitted with a catalytic converter accelerates hard or is under a heavy load climbing a hill.

_____

14 If your vehicle breaks down on the motorway would you put a warning triangle on the road?

　a No.
　b Yes.
　c Yes, but only on the hard shoulder.

15 Look at Fig. 3 and Fig. 4 on Plate D. Which is the steeper gradient? The one going downhill or the one going uphill?

_____

16 Name four groups of people who cannot use a motorway.

_____

_____

_____

_____

17 Look at Fig. 5 on Plate D. On what motorway can you find these services?

_____

18 You are travelling on a motorway when you see a flashing amber sign on the central reservation with a speed of 50 mph. Is this speed advisory or mandatory?

_____

19 Which one of the following does the *Driving Manual* advise you to check daily?
a Speedometer.
b Mirrors.
c Horn.
d Brakes.

20 Motorcycles with less than 50 cc engine capacity are still legal with a tyre tread of less than 1 mm if the base of any groove from the original tread can still be seen. True or false?

_____

21 The *Highway Code* recommends that where there is no pavement or footpath pedestrians should

   a walk on the right-hand side so that they can see oncoming traffic ☐

   b walk on the left-hand side of the road to avoid head-on collisions ☐

   c not worry about which side of the road they are on but take care ☐

22 You are driving on the motorway and see serious congestion ahead of you. What can you do that might reduce the risk of a rear-end collision?

23 Vehicle Excise Duty is graduated in two bands of engine size. A reduced rate of £100 is charged if you own a vehicle with what size engine?

24 Is it compulsory to carry a first aid kit in your car in the Czech Republic?

25 Look at Fig. 6 on Plate D. In which seaside town are you likely to find this sign and what does it mean?

26 You are approaching a stop sign at the end of a road. The correct method of changing gears from 5th to 1st is to come through the gear box from 5th to 4th to 3rd to 2nd to 1st. True or false?

27 A vehicle's radiator is likely to overheat where

a too much coolant has been used ☐

b not enough coolant has been used ☐

c the ignition timing has been advanced
  too far ☐

d the ignition timing has been excessively
  retarded ☐

28 Is it compulsory to carry a first aid kit in your
  car in Denmark?

_____

29 Is the wearing of rear seat belts compulsory in
  all European countries?

_____

30 When an oncoming vehicle is approaching you
  on a single track road with the passing place on
  your left, you should

a pull into the passing place ☐

b wait opposite the passing place ☐

c stop immediately ☐

d keep moving ☐

31 What does DETR stand for?

_____

32 Look at Fig. 7 on Plate D and imagine you are
  driving a car along this road. What will the
  speed limit be as you pass the road sign?

_____

33 Are passengers allowed to ride in a caravan whilst it's being towed?

_____

34 When turning right from a narrow side road, a driver should position the vehicle

a well over to the left ☐
b just left of the centre of the road ☐
c just over the centre of the road ☐
d in the middle of the road ☐

35 What percentage of drivers never take any further driving tuition after passing their driving test?

_____

36 When was the Theory Test for drivers of large vehicles updated?

_____

37 What is the blood alcohol legal limit at which you may drive a car in Italy?

_____

38 You are driving in the left-hand lane of a motorway. You see a number of vehicles merging from a slip road ahead. You should

a increase your speed to get ahead of them ☐
b leave it to the other vehicles to adjust their speed ☐
c continue at the national speed limit ☐
d be ready to move to the centre lane ☐

39 If you break down on the hard shoulder of the motorway which would be the safest way to face the wheels of your vehicle?

_____

40 What is the blood alcohol legal limit at which you may drive a car in Switzerland?

_____

Total score for Test 4 _____

45

SECTION ONE
TEST 5

1 When a driver is likely to be stationary at a road junction for some time, the recommended procedure is to

   a keep the footbrake applied and select neutral ☐

   b keep the footbrake applied and select first gear ☐

   c select neutral and apply the handbrake ☐

   d apply the handbrake and select neutral ☐

2 Look at Fig. 1 on Plate E. What would the sign indicate to you as a driver of a Large Goods Vehicle?

_____

3 Is it legal to ride your bicycle along the pavement?

_____

4 You are driving at night on a motorway. You have your headlights on main beam. When are you particularly likely to dazzle oncoming drivers?

_____

5 Look at Fig. 2 on Plate E. Can you identify this sign?

_____

6 You are driving on a quiet stretch of a three-lane motorway at 70 mph. Would you

  a stay in the left-hand lane as much as possible? ☐

  b stay in the middle lane as much as possible? ☐

  c stay in the right-hand lane as much as possible? ☐

7 What colour reflective studs are used to mark contraflow systems and road works on motorways?

_____

8 What is the name given to a temporary motorway system where traffic travelling in the opposite direction shares the same carriageway?

_____

9 The purpose of the camber in the road is to

  a help drainage ☐

  b provide banking which assists steering ☐

  c provide an angle of slope towards the centre of the road ☐

  d assist fatigued drivers to pull over to the left ☐

10 Which brake on your motorcycle is the most powerful and the most important?

_____

11 What is 'Pass Plus'?

_____

12 Are British tourists travelling across Europe exempt from paying toll fees?

_____

13 What do the letters IAM stand for?

_____

14 On toucan crossings, cyclists

   a are permitted to walk across the road

   b are permitted to ride across the road

   c may proceed when the road is clear of traffic

15 Look at Fig. 3 on Plate E. As a driver what would you see next?

_____

16 What is the shortest stopping distance in metres at 70 mph?

_____

17 Look at Fig. 4 on Plate E and imagine that you are driving a car on this road. What is the speed limit?

_____

18 Is it compulsory to carry a first aid kit in your car in Belgium?

_____

19 When checking the tyre pressures before making a long journey at high speeds, a driver may need to

   a double the pressure in the front tyres only

   b double the pressure in the rear tyres only

   c increase the pressures

20 Do signals on the central reservation of a motorway only apply to those vehicles using the right-hand lane?

_____

21 When a pedestrian is standing on the pavement with one foot on a zebra crossing, a driver

   a must assume that the pedestrian is about to cross the road

   b should stop, providing there is no following traffic

   c should assume that the pedestrian will wait before crossing

22 Is it compulsory to carry a first aid kit in your car in Croatia?

_____

23 You are on the M6. You have been on the motorway for about an hour travelling at high speed. What must you be aware of in relation to your speed when you leave the motorway?

_____

_____

24 How many metres before the start of the motorway slip road are countdown markers placed?

_____

25 Look at Fig. 5 on Plate E. Where would you see this sign and what does it mean?

_____

_____

26 Where must GB or EU plates be displayed on your vehicle when driving abroad?

_____

27 The differential enables a vehicle to be driven round a bend with the

a driven wheels turning at the same speed ☐

b inside wheel turning faster than the outside wheel ☐

c outside wheel turning faster than the inside wheel ☐

d transmission disengaged without loss of speed ☐

28 Where are the only parking places provided on a motorway?

_____

29 You are driving towards an unmanned level crossing. You see a red light flashing, but the barrier doesn't come down. What should you do?

_____

30 Which procedure will a police officer in a patrol vehicle use to stop you?

   a Flash the headlights, point to the left and use the left indicator. ☐

   b Use the siren, overtake, cut in front and stop. ☐

   c Pull alongside, use the siren and wave you to stop. ☐

31 What is the blood alcohol legal limit at which you may drive a car in Hungary?

_____

32 Look at Fig. 6 on Plate E. As a driver what would you see next?

_____

33 What is a hazcem card and where would you see it being displayed?

_____

_____

34 After overtaking another vehicle how would you know it was safe to move back into the left?

   a When the other driver uses the hazard warning lights as a signal. ☐

   b By waiting for the driver you have just overtaken to flash the headlight. ☐

   c By checking your interior and nearside mirrors. ☐

   d By checking your interior and offside mirrors. ☐

35 What is the blood alcohol legal limit at which you may drive a car in the Republic of Ireland?

_____

36 If you were driving a Large Goods Vehicle when would you use an endurance (retarder) brake?

_____

37 What do the letters RoSPA stand for?

_____

38 You are driving on a motorway. Before you overtake you should check for any vehicles in the right-hand mirror that might be about to

  a leave the motorway

  b move back to the left

  c cut in sharply behind you

  d overtake you

39 You are driving a Passenger Carrying Vehicle (PCV) and the conductor rings the bell four times. What does this mean?

_____

40 What is the shortest stopping distance in metres at 50 mph?

_____

Total score for Test 5 _____

SECTION TWO
TEST 6

1 When changing up gear you will need to depress the clutch

  a first, and then lift your right foot off the accelerator ☐

  b and lift your right foot off the accelerator at the same time ☐

  c and keep your right foot on the accelerator ☐

  d after lifting your right foot off the accelerator ☐

2 Look at Fig. 1 on Plate F. The motorcyclist is in the process of taking his DSA motorbike test. Would he incur a rider error for the positioning around this bend?

       _____

3 CBT (Compulsory Basic Training) was introduced in 1990. For what reason was it introduced?

_____

4 You should always adapt your driving to suit the type and condition of road you are on, particularly anticipating unexpected or difficult situations. What precaution would you take approaching a blind bend and why?

_____

_____

5 What does Fig. 2 on Plate F mean?

_____

6 Carrying a warning triangle is compulsory in most European countries for all vehicles with more than two wheels. True or false?

_____

7 Imagine you are driving along a national speed limit single carriageway road, making good progress. You are following another vehicle and are maintaining an adequate safety gap. The car behind you overtakes and pulls into the gap in front of you. What should you do?

_____

8 When you are driving and the roads are icy you should avoid sudden actions as these can cause a skid. You should, for example, accelerate and brake very gently. How else could you drive to help keep your vehicle under control?

_____

_____

9 Traffic signs giving directions on a motorway have a

a blue background with white letters

b blue background with black letters

c yellow background with black letters

d green background with white letters

10 You are moving away on a very steep downhill gradient. What should you do?

a Select second gear, firmly brake, release the handbrake and move off when it is safe.

b Select first gear, bring the clutch to the biting point and move off when it is safe.

c Select first gear, firmly brake, release the handbrake and move off when it is safe.

11 From the following list of attitudes, pick three which predispose you to risk.

a Enjoying the thrill of danger.

b Justifying risks because they are taken in a noble cause.

c Overestimating your own ability.

d A good level of attention.

e Acting to keep identified risks to a minimum.

f Skilful use of vehicle controls.

12 Whilst riding, in good conditions, along a normal two-way road, a motorcycle rider chooses to overtake a line of moving vehicles. There is no oncoming traffic. Of which two things should the motorcyclist be aware to reduce the risk of a crash?

_____

_____

13 Certain attitudes may undermine safe driving
practices. Pick three of these from the following
list.

a Valuing speed and competitiveness.

b Courtesy.

c An obvious concern for safety.

d Using aggressive language.

e An overemphasis on reaching
destinations on time.

14 You are about to move the car away. You
prepare the car to move and check all around
you. There are no other vehicles or pedestrians.
You should

a give a right-hand signal, release the
handbrake, have a final look round and
move away

b release the handbrake, have a final look
round and move away

c release the handbrake, have a final look
round, signal right and move away

15 Look at Fig. 3 on Plate F. What are these
signs?

_____

16 If you were driving defensively in the following
situation what would you have done wrong?
You are about to park the car on the left-hand
side of the road. You see that there is no need to
signal, you gently brake and steer into your
parking place. Before the car stops, you select

neutral and, when the car has stopped, you apply the handbrake and switch off the ignition.

_____

_____

_____

17 Look at Fig. 4 on Plate F. Is this man breaking the law?

_____

18 When speed is doubled what happens to the braking distance?

_____

19 The cause of excessive wear to the outside edges of a tyre is most likely to be

a over inflation
b under inflation
c uneven road conditions
d defective speed humps

20 Which three things does the *Highway Code* state about carrying passengers on motorcycles, in addition to safety helmets and suitable clothing?

_____

_____

_____

21 You are driving along a road with cars parked on both sides and there is another vehicle approaching. The road is not wide enough for both of you. You should

   a check your mirrors and slow down, looking for a safe gap to steer into ☐

   b keep going as the oncoming vehicle will probably give way to you ☐

   c flash your headlights and steer into a gap on the left-hand side of the road ☐

22 If you are travelling at 50 mph, leaving a two-second time gap between you and the vehicle in front, how big is the gap in metres?

_____

23 What is the maximum speed capability of powered vehicles used by disabled people?

_____

24 Name three factors that affect your stopping distance.

_____

_____

_____

25 What does Fig. 5 on Plate F mean?

_____

26 You are driving in Wales and are following a vehicle with a red 'D' plate displayed on the front and rear of the vehicle. What does this mean?

_____

27 Constant velocity (cv) joints are part of a front-wheel drive vehicle's

   a transmission

   b suspension

   c steering

   d tracking

28 It is illegal to refuse to insure a person to drive a car, increase the premium or reduce the level of cover, on the basis of a person's disability. Which act outlaws discrimination against disabled people in this way, and when was it introduced?

_____

_____

29 Your vehicle is over three years old. When is the only time you are allowed to drive your vehicle without a current M.O.T. certificate?

_____

30 Just before turning right from a main road to a side road, you should check your offside mirror. This is because

   a there may be pedestrians stepping into the road

   b you need to check your road position

   c a motorcyclist may be overtaking you

   d you can never trust the interior mirror

31 What is RAMP?

_____

32 Look at Fig. 6 on Plate F. Should this driver be overtaking the cyclist?

_____

33 When driving a large goods vehicle, a loud buzzer sounds in the cab. What is this most likely to be?

_____

34 Another vehicle has overtaken you and has pulled in too close in front. You should

a slow down
b drive on close behind
c overtake the vehicle
d flash your headlights

35 What is the minimum age that someone would be able to qualify for an Orange or Blue Badge?

_____

36 You are driving a slow-moving vehicle and see a circular sign showing a white 30 on a blue background. What does this sign mean?

_____

37 Which European country has no concessionary parking scheme for disabled motorists?

_____

38 You are driving on a three-lane motorway. You are about to move into the middle lane to overtake a slower vehicle. You should check

  a for traffic in the right-hand lane returning to the middle lane ☐

  b for traffic which is intending to leave at the next exit ☐

  c the nearside mirror before pulling out ☐

  d for any traffic behind that is trying to pass you on the left ☐

39 If you are driving either a Large Goods Vehicle (LGV) or a Passenger Carrying Vehicle (PCV) under normal conditions, when is it acceptable to straddle lanes?

_____

40 The Road Traffic Act 1988 provides scope for seat belt exemption for some disabled people. There is no specific list of reasons which would automatically exempt an individual, so how is the decision made?

_____

Total score for Test 6 _____

44

SECTION TWO
TEST 7

1 Missing out gears when changing speed

   a is preferable, but not recommended ☐

   b can be harmful to the engine and gear box ☐

   c can be just as safe as changing through the gears one by one ☐

   d is only acceptable when making block changes down ☐

2 Look at Fig. 1 on Plate G. If you were driving this vehicle and saw the motorcycle in your nearside door mirror, of what should you be aware?

_____

3 If you were travelling through Germany on your motorbike, you would find that the practice of riding two abreast is 'Verboten'. True or false?

_____

4 If you were driving defensively in the following situation what would you have done wrong? You are moving away on a steep downhill gradient. You select first gear, bring the clutch to the biting point and move off when it is safe.

_____

5 Imagine you are following the vehicle shown in Fig. 2 on Plate G. What is the driver indicating to you with this arm signal?

_____

6 You are driving on a national speed limit single carriageway. The road is bending round to the left ahead of you and the high hedges mean that you cannot see around the bend. Would you

a position well to the left?

b position just left of centre?

c position well to the right?

7 If you were driving defensively in the following situation what would you have done wrong? You are about to move the car away. You prepare the car to move and check all around you. There are no other vehicles or pedestrians so you give a right-hand signal, release the handbrake, have a final look round and move away.

_____

_____

8 On a dual carriageway powered vehicles used by a disabled person must have a flashing amber light because their maximum speed is so low. What is the maximum speed at which one of these vehicles will travel?

_____

9 The likelihood of skidding on snow is reduced where a driver selects

a second gear ☐
b a low gear ☐
c the highest possible gear ☐
d rear wheel drive ☐

10 What type of motorcycle can you ride if you hold a licence with the A1 category on it?

11 If you are not one of the first to arrive at the scene of an accident and enough people have already stopped to give assistance, what should you do?

12 Cycle lanes are marked with white lines (that may be broken) along the carriageway. True or false?

13 What is the more common name for an ambulance driver who has had Extended Ambulance Aid training?

14 You approach the end of the road intending to turn left. It is a crossroads and the driver opposite is indicating an intention to turn right. Would you

a go first as it is your priority? ☐
b make eye contact as there is no priority? ☐
c let the other driver go first as it is their priority? ☐

15 Look at Fig. 3 on Plate G. Does the sign mean 'Ahead only' or 'One-way street'?

_____

16 Vehicles carrying dangerous goods in packages will be marked with colour reflective plates of which colour?

_____

17 Look at Fig. 4 on Plate G. The motorist has just overtaken the cyclist. Is that legal?

_____

18 Switzerland applies a limit to the weight of roof rack loads. What is this limit?

_____

19 What is the correct procedure for stopping a vehicle equipped with an anti-lock braking system in an emergency?

a Apply the footbrake firmly in a pumping action until the vehicle has stopped. ☐

b Apply the footbrake continuously until the vehicle has stopped. ☐

c Apply the footbrake and handbrake until the vehicle has stopped. ☐

d Apply the handbrake only. ☐

20 Under the penalty point system (January 2001), a driver who accumulates 12 points within a three-year period will be faced with what?

_____

21 Large vehicles can block your view of the road ahead. How can you improve your ability to see and plan ahead?

a Flash the driver letting him know that he should pull over for you.

b Overtake as soon as you can.

c Pull back to increase your separation distance.

22 There are seven service stations on the M1 between Leeds and Leicester. Name them.

_____

_____

_____

_____

_____

_____

_____

23 What is meant by 'kick down' when driving a vehicle fitted with automatic transmission?

_____

24 The sequence of lights at some pedestrian crossings is red, flashing amber, green, amber, red. Name three pedestrian crossings which do not conform to this sequence.

_____

_____

_____

25 Look at Fig. 5 on Plate G. Imagine you are driving a car along a country road and see this sign. What is the maximum speed at which you can drive on this road?

_____

26 It is an offence to combine cross-ply and radial-ply tyres in a certain way on your vehicle. What is that way?

_____

27 Just before moving away a driver needs to look round over the right shoulder

  a because there may be another road user in the blindspot ☐

  b to check the offside mirror for a wider field of view ☐

  c to check that it is safe to signal ☐

28 What is the maximum fine the court can impose for careless or inconsiderate driving?

_____

29 How can you tell whether or not the shock absorbers on your car are worn?

_____

30 When emerging at a crossroads where it is necessary to give way, drivers must give way to traffic approaching from

  a ahead only ☐

  b the right only ☐

  c the left only ☐

  d the right and left ☐

31 Name the device designed to convert mechanical energy into electrical energy.

_____

32 Look at Fig. 6 on Plate G. If the speed limit is 30 mph on this road, what is the overall stopping distance likely to be?

_____

33 Why is it important to distribute the weight evenly over the axles when loading a large goods vehicle?

_____

34 You are approaching a working snowplough on a motorway. You should consider not overtaking because

  a it is illegal to overtake snowploughs ☐
  b snowploughs are left-hand drive only ☐
  c your speed could cause snow to drift behind ☐
  d there may be deep snow ahead ☐

35 Modern cars most commonly have four valves per cylinder. So a four-cylinder engine would be a '16-valve' engine. What purpose would these four valves serve?

_____

36 You are driving a Passenger Carrying Vehicle (PCV) and you experience a front wheel blow out. What is the first thing you should do?

_____

37 Name the devices fitted to diesel engines to help start the engine from cold and to reduce smoke immediately after start-up.

_____

38 When re-joining the left-hand lane of a motorway from the hard shoulder after dealing with a vehicle breakdown a driver should

  a wait for a gap in the traffic ☐

  b signal right and then re-join the left lane ☐

  c build up speed on the hard shoulder and watch for a safe gap in the traffic ☐

  d carefully build up speed using the hazard warning lights ☐

39 Within how many days, under European Rules, must completed tachograph charts be handed into employers?

_____

40 What is the term for the group of components which transmits power from the car's engine to the driven road wheels?

_____

Total score for Test 7 _____

48

SECTION TWO
TEST 8

1 When turning a corner at speed, the weight of a vehicle is transferred towards the

   a vehicle's nearside
   b vehicle's offside
   c inside of the curve
   d outside of the curve

2 Look at Fig. 1 on Plate H. The lorry is parked at the side of the road. Are the vehicles overtaking the lorry committing an offence?

_____

3 You are riding a motorcycle and carrying a pillion passenger. What might you have to do to your tyres?

_____

4 According to the latest research fatigue may be the principal factor in what percentage of all driving accidents?

_____

5 Fig. 2 on Plate H is seen on a dashboard of a car with a diesel engine. What does it mean?

_____

6 You are about to move away from the side of the road. There is not a safe gap to pull into because of the traffic on the road. Should you give a right-hand signal?

   a Yes, a signal informs other road users of your intentions to pull out.

   b Yes, a signal might encourage someone to let you out.

   c No, a signal may mislead other road users.

7 What does BITER stand for?

_____

8 In Northern Ireland the R Driver Scheme restricts speeds for the first year after passing the driving test. To what speed are R Drivers restricted?

_____

9 When cornering on snow or ice you should travel round

   a with a high engine speed

   b at a steady speed in a high gear

   c in a low gear

   d in neutral

10 The rear wheel of a motorcycle could be driven by any one of three things. Can you identify all three?

_____

_____

_____

11 Pass Plus is a course designed for drivers who have recently passed their driving test. On completion of the course a certificate will be issued. Who issues the certificate?

_____

12 You have just had two new tyres fitted to your motorbike. As new tyres have a shininess that reduces grip on the road, approximately how far should you ride carefully before the shininess wears off?

_____

13 The effects of one pint of beer on a person wear off after half an hour. True or false?

_____

14 You are about to turn right into a side road. In judging a safe gap in the traffic, what would your main consideration be?

a Whether you can keep the car moving in second gear. ☐

b Whether you can complete the turn without causing anyone to slow down or change direction because of you. ☐

c Whether someone is going to flash the headlights to let you go. ☐

15 Look at Fig. 3 on Plate H. If the pedestrian sees this, what does the driver see?

_____

16 Statistics show that drivers tend to repeat the types of crashes they have. True or false?

_____

17 Look at Fig. 4 and Fig. 5 on Plate H. Is the van positioned correctly?

_____

18 Why is it preferable to use an emergency telephone on the motorway to your own mobile phone, if you have an incident to report to the police?

_____

19 When the fan belt in a vehicle's engine is slipping, a driver will notice that

a the battery is flat

b the engine has stalled

c there will be more noise under the bonnet

20 You are buying a second-hand car and on the description it states the vehicle has P.A.S. What does P.A.S stand for?

_____

21 Which option below best defines a driving hazard?

a A hazard is something which appears suddenly in front of you.

b A hazard is something which cannot be avoided.

c A hazard is something which might cause you to change speed or direction.

22 To which lanes do signals situated on the central reservation of a motorway apply?

_____

23 Carrying a green card whilst driving abroad is a statutory requirement in most EU countries. True or false?

_____

24 Name the device that consists of the following five components: the friction disc, the pressure plate, the diaphragm spring, the cover, the release bearing.

_____

25 Look at Fig. 6 on Plate H. What can you do when you see this sign?

_____

26 Countdown markers are seen on motorways before exits. What distance is there between each marker and what colour are they?

_____

27 What should a driver do when another vehicle is following too closely?

   a Use the two-second rule. ☐
   b Speed up to increase the gap with the vehicle behind. ☐
   c Slow down slightly to increase the distance with any vehicle in front. ☐
   d Touch the brake to tell the driver to slow down. ☐

28 Name the system engine management systems usually have, which is used to store details of any faults, allowing these faults to be traced quickly and easily.

_____

29 What do amber flashing lights mean when seen on a motorway sign?

_____

30 The safest way to pass other vehicles when turning right at a road junction is

a offside to offside

b nearside to nearside

c offside to nearside

d nearside to offside

31 Double-overhead camshaft engines have two camshafts. What do these two camshafts operate?

_____

32 Look at Fig. 7 on Plate H. Is the driver of the red car coming towards us doing anything wrong?

_____

33 You are driving a Passenger Carrying Vehicle. You park in a safe place and leave the vehicle unattended with the engine switched off and all the doors locked. What must you ensure?

_____

34 A driver of a Large Goods Vehicle is trying to overtake you on a two-lane dual carriageway. What should you do?

- **a** Increase your speed and force the lorry to drop back.
- **b** Hold the same speed.
- **c** Be prepared to reduce your speed.
- **d** Brake hard to allow the other driver to cut in.

35 Before starting a motorway journey you should run through a POWER check. What do these letters stand for?

_____

36 Large Goods Vehicles (LGV), by law have to display a hazard warning plate when transporting hazardous goods. You can determine their cargo by the information displayed on the plate. If they were carrying dangerous goods, what would you expect to see displayed on the plate?

_____

37 Name the device installed in the exhaust system that converts harmful by-products of combustion into carbon dioxide and water vapour by means of a heat-producing chemical reaction.

_____

38 The advice given in the *Highway Code*, immediately on leaving a motorway, is that drivers should check the

a interior mirror
b offside mirror
c speedometer
d brakes and gears

39 The driver of a Passenger Carrying Vehicle requires a licence to carry paying passengers. What is this licence called?

_____

40 Who has set the maximum penalties for road traffic offences?

_____

Total score for Test 8 _____

43

SECTION TWO
TEST 9

1 When intending to turn a corner where there is loose gravel on the road a driver should

   a reduce the vehicle's speed in plenty of time ☐

   b steer round the corner maintaining stability under firm acceleration ☐

   c use a low gear with a high engine speed ☐

   d use a high gear with a high engine speed ☐

2 Look at Fig. 1 on Plate I. Is this vehicle breaking the law by cutting the right-hand corner on this right turn?

_____

3 You are riding your motorcycle. What is known as a 'life saver check' before joining a motorway from the slip road?

_____

4 If you were driving defensively in the following situation what would you have done wrong? You are about to emerge left at the end of the road. Your vision on the approach to the give way lines is good. You check right and can see the road to the right is clear. You select second gear and emerge to the left.

_____

5 Look at Fig. 2 on Plate I. If this sign appears whilst you are driving, what might it indicate?

_____

6 You are driving at 60 mph on a country road. There is a sharp bend ahead of you. Would you

a slow down and change down before the bend and accelerate gently around the bend? ☐

b change down before the bend without braking and accelerate around the bend? ☐

c slow down in the bend and change down after the bend is finished? ☐

7 If you were driving defensively in the following situation what would you have done wrong? You are travelling along a national speed limit single carriageway road. There seems to be a problem on the road ahead. The vehicle in front is braking hard. You start braking and briefly switch on your hazard warning lights to warn following traffic of a hazard ahead.

_____

_____

8 What is the name of the certificate required to qualify someone as an ambulance driver?

_____

9 The engine of a vehicle fitted with automatic transmission can be started when the selector is positioned in

  a drive
  b neutral only
  c park or neutral
  d 1, 2 or 3

10 When riding your motorcycle on a motorway you should be particularly aware of the weather conditions. Name three of the most common weather problems you could encounter.

_____

_____

_____

11 In Germany does traffic on a roundabout have priority over traffic entering?

_____

12 You are driving along a motorway. You see a red flashing light above your lane. What does it mean?

_____

13 Name the motorway services nearest to Cheddar Gorge.

_____

14 It is generally acknowledged that the majority of road accidents are caused by

   a mechanical or tyre failures

   b poor weather conditions

   c human error

15 Look at Fig. 3 on Plate I. Name two locations where you might expect to see this sign.

_____

_____

16 A prominent red flag should be attached to anything extending more than a certain distance beyond the car's rear bumper. What is that distance?

_____

17 Look at Fig. 4 on Plate I. If you use the left-hand lane through the road works, will you automatically be taken off at the next junction?

_____

18 Name the two most effective ways to counter sleepiness when driving, suggested by the *Highway Code*.

_____

_____

19 While travelling past traffic at 70 mph on a two-lane dual carriageway, a car with its headlights flashing comes up quickly behind. You should

a to avoid baulking, move over to let the car pass straight away ☐

b move over to let the car pass as soon as safely possible ☐

c touch the footbrake gently to tell the driver to slow down ☐

d take no action and not be intimidated ☐

20 Driving too slowly for the road and traffic conditions, and hesitation, causing insufficient progress, are two of the most common failure points in the practical driving test for car drivers. Which one is the more common reason for failure?

_____

21 It is permissible to overtake on the left

a on a fast dual carriageway or motorway ☐

b when the driver ahead is turning right and has signalled this intention and there is room down the left-hand side ☐

c within the zig-zag lines of a pedestrian crossing ☐

22 At any time, the police have the power to require a driver to take an eyesight test in good daylight. What is the legal distance from which you would be required to read a number plate?

_____

23 When did the changes to the driving test take place that included the introduction of a maximum 15 driver faults before failing the test?

_____

24 Should you use a warning triangle if your vehicle has broken down on the motorway?

_____

25 Look at Fig. 5 on Plate I. What does this symbol mean?

_____

26 You are travelling towards a zebra crossing with a central refuge. There are pedestrians waiting to cross from the left. You

a should give way and wait until the pedestrians have reached the other side of the road before driving on ☐

b should give way and wait until the pedestrians have reached the central refuge before driving on ☐

c should not give way as they have not started to cross the road ☐

27 When turning right from a side road on to a lightly trafficked dual carriageway with a wide central reservation a driver should

a treat each carriageway as two separate roads ☐

b wait until both carriageways are clear before emerging ☐

c turn left and find an alternative route ☐

d edge out slowly so other traffic will see you ☐

28 How many penalty points over what period lead to a disqualification?

_____

29 You are driving along a road in a built-up area. There are houses and parked vehicles on both sides. Name four potential hazards.

_____   _____

_____   _____

30 When driving at night a driver should

    a use side lights only in a built-up area

    b use side lights only outside a built-up area

    c use full beam in a built-up area

    d be able to stop within the range of the headlamps

31 What is the maximum term of imprisonment the courts can impose for causing death by dangerous driving?

_____

32 Look at Fig. 6 on Plate I. Is the red car ahead positioned incorrectly?

_____

33 Who is responsible for issuing tachograph charts to drivers of Large Goods Vehicles (LGV) and Passenger Carrying Vehicles (PCV)?

_____

34 When leaving a motorway you are likely to think that your vehicle's speed is

    a less than it really is

    b more than it really is

    c exactly as you feel it is

35 Name the mechanically driven device on an engine responsible for electrically firing the spark plug at a pre-determined point of the piston stroke.

_____

36 On a double-decker bus, what depth of tyre tread is required over three-quarters of the tyre's width?

_____

37 Black smoke from the exhaust is often caused by too much fuel in the fuel/air mixture. What could this damage very quickly if the car has a catalytic converter fitted?

_____

38 Driving examiners undergo an intensive training course. Where is this course conducted?

_____

39 You are driving a PCV. What is a 'Splitter box'?

_____

40 Name the device, which allows a smooth transfer of power from the engine to the transmission when moving the car away from a standstill, and when changing gear.

_____

Total score for Test 9 _____

SECTION TWO
TEST 10

1 When parking facing uphill on the left-hand side of the road next to the kerb, drivers are advised to leave their vehicles with the front wheels

   a turned to the left
   b turned to the right
   c straight with the handbrake applied
   d straight and the gear lever in neutral

2 Look at Fig. 1 on Plate J. In front of what sort of building is the car parked and should it be there?

_____

3 You are on holiday and visiting the UK from Spain. Can you ride your motorbike in the UK on your Spanish licence?

_____

4 If you were driving defensively in the following situation what would you have done wrong?
You are driving along a road with cars parked on both sides of the road and there is another vehicle approaching. The road is not wide enough for both of you. You flash your headlights and steer into a gap on the left-hand side of the road. As soon as the approaching vehicle passes you proceed.

_____

5 Identify Fig. 2 on Plate J.

_____

6 The shape of signs is important. For example, circular signs

   a provide warnings ☐
   b give orders ☐
   c give information ☐

7 You are driving up to the traffic lights ahead of you, which are on red. You need to start slowing down. You use the MSM routine. What does the 'S' stand for and, in this instance, which 'S' would you be using?

_____

_____

8 Name two instances when you must not use your horn.

_____

_____

9 The transmission in an automatic vehicle responds to changes in the

   a driving style only ☐
   b engine's load only ☐
   c vehicle's road speed and traffic conditions ☐
   d vehicle's road speed and load on the engine ☐

10 Identify two things a bicycle rider should consider to improve their safety when travelling along in foggy conditions in the daytime.

_____

_____

11 'Should' you, or 'must' you stop at a stop sign?

_____

12 You are following a cyclist along a road and you see them look over their right shoulder. What could you expect their next move to be?

_____

13 Is it illegal to reverse out of a driveway on to the main road?

_____

14 Drivers approaching a red light signal at a puffin crossing should anticipate the red light signal

a being followed by a flashing amber signal ☐
b being followed by a steady amber signal only ☐
c staying at red while pedestrians are using the crossing ☐

15 Look at Fig. 3 on Plate J. Is this temporary speed limit sign mandatory or advisory?

_____

16 Front or rear fog lights should only be used when visibility is seriously reduced to what distance?

_____

17 Look at Fig. 4 on Plate J. and decide 'should' you or 'must' you give way to these pedestrians?

_____

18 What requirements must you fulfil to supervise a learner car driver?

_____

_____

19 Overinflated tyres will become worn

a in the centre first
b at the outside edges first
c unevenly
d evenly

20 Which side of the road should British drivers drive on in Spain?

_____

21 When you park facing down a steep hill you should

a keep as far away from the kerb as possible
b keep your front wheels straight
c turn your front wheels towards the kerb

22 Name two occasions when you must show your motor insurance certificate.

_____

_____

23 Why is unleaded petrol more environmentally
friendly?

_____

24 For registration documents issued after 27 March
1997 the buyer and seller are responsible for
completing the registration documents. Who is
responsible for forwarding them to the DVLA?

_____

25 Look at Fig. 5 on Plate J and imagine you are
driving a Large Goods Vehicle when you see this
sign. What action would you take?

_____

26 You parked your car on a road at night with
street lighting and no signs indicating a speed
limit. Must you display parking lights?

_____

27 If when driving you have to warn someone of
your presence, in what conditions would flashing
the headlights be the most appropriate signal?

   a In hazy mist conditions.

   b In slow-moving dense traffic.

   c On fast roads where the noise level is high.

   d Driving over speed humps in residential
      areas.

28 What must a vehicle display if it is exempt from
Vehicle Excise Duty?

_____

29 You are involved in an accident where you need to give first aid. The *Highway Code* gives a brief outline of emergency care. Part of the outline consists of A, B & C. What do these letters stand for?

_____

_____

_____

30 You are turning right on to a dual carriageway from a side road. Your vehicle is too long for the central gap. How should you proceed?

  a Move forward and wait in the middle.
  b Wait until it is clear from both directions.
  c Edge out slowly so other traffic will see you.
  d Turn left and find an alternative route.

31 New drivers, who commit driving offences, risk having their licence revoked and will then have to reapply for a provisional licence and pass the theory and the practical tests again. How many points over what period will lead to this situation?

_____

32 Look at Fig. 6 on Plate J. If you parked your car to the right of this sign on Tuesday morning at 7 am, should you be surprised to come back and find a parking ticket on the windscreen?

_____

33 Where would you find details of the weight your vehicle can tow?

_____

34 A driver will need to dip the headlights earlier when approaching and driving around a

a left-hand bend

b right-hand bend

35 What are the penalties for using faulty tyres worn beyond the minimum legal tread depth?

_____

_____

36 You are driving a large high-sided vehicle across a viaduct and are about to overtake a motorcyclist. As you pass you allow plenty of room. What should you check and for what reason, after you have passed them?

_____

_____

37 In order to pass the driving technique part of the driving instructor's qualifying examination you are required to take an eyesight test, which involves you being able to read a number plate in good daylight from a distance of 20.5 metres. True or false?

_____

38 When travelling down a motorway deceleration
lane a driver should

   a check the speedometer and adjust the
vehicle's speed

   b keep up with the traffic flow in the
deceleration lane

   c keep at the national speed limit

39 Why is it inadvisable to drive three abreast on a
three-lane dual carriageway?

_____

40 What is the maximum fine the court can impose
for no M.O.T. certificate on a car?

_____

Total score for Test 10 ____

45

1 When parking facing downhill on the left-hand side of the road next to the kerb, drivers are advised to leave their vehicles with the handbrake applied and select

   a reverse gear with the front wheels turned to the left ☐

   b reverse gear with the front wheels turned to the right ☐

   c first gear with the front wheels turned to the right ☐

   d neutral with the front wheels turned ahead ☐

2 Look at Fig. 1 on Plate K and give two reasons why the motorcyclist should not have parked there.

   _____

   _____

3 You are following a cyclist, who extends her left arm out horizontally. What is she intending to do?

   _____

4 If you have had a crash in one three-year period, how much more likely are you to have another similar crash in the next three years?

---

5 Look at Fig. 2 on Plate K. What does this sign mean?

---

6 You are driving on an urban dual carriageway. The speed limit is 40 mph and you are travelling at the maximum speed for the road. The weather and road conditions are good and there is some following traffic. Ahead of you the lights have just changed to red. You should

  a check your mirrors, select a lower gear and brake to a stop ☐

  b check your mirrors and gently brake to a stop ☐

  c check your mirrors and slowly apply the handbrake ☐

7 Two of the most common failure points in the practical driving test for car drivers are not making effective use of the mirrors well before changing direction and incorrect use of the controls when reversing. Which one is the more common reason for failure?

---

8 What is the maximum fine the court can impose for traffic light offences?

---

9 The *Driving Manual* recommends that when driving a car fitted with automatic transmission the

a right foot should be used to operate both the accelerator and the footbrake ☐

b right foot should be used to operate the accelerator and the footbrake when manoeuvring ☐

c left foot should never be used to operate the footbrake ☐

d footbrake only need be used to check creep when waiting ☐

10 What colour is the cycle symbol 'to go' at cycle-only crossings?

_____

11 What is the maximum term of imprisonment the courts can impose for driving when disqualified?

_____

12 If you intend riding a motorcycle at night, what should your two most important considerations be regarding visibility?

_____

_____

13 What colour reflective road studs mark the left edge of the road?

_____

14 It is raining and you are travelling in heavy traffic. The vehicle behind you is getting too close. What should you do?

 a Increase the gap between you and the vehicle in front until there is at least a four-second time gap. ☐

 b Increase the gap between you and the vehicle in front until there is at least a two-second time gap. ☐

 c Speed up slightly to increase the gap between you and the vehicle behind. ☐

15 Look at Fig. 3 on Plate K. Does the sign mean 'road narrows on both sides' or 'end of dual carriageway'?

_____

16 What is the blood alcohol legal limit at which you may drive a car in Germany?

_____

17 Look at Fig. 4 on Plate K. If it were dark the driver of this white car would have done at least three things wrong. What would they be? (The question carries a maximum of three points.)

_____

_____

_____

18 Is it compulsory to carry a first aid kit in your car in Sweden?

_____

19 Higher tyre pressures will be an advantage when

   a driving long distances at high speeds ☐
   b driving on rough road surfaces ☐
   c most driving is in town ☐
   d using cross-ply tyres ☐

20 What is meant by an 'adverse' camber?

_____

21 You are travelling in fourth gear at 40 mph, the speed limit for the road. The road ahead slopes steeply down for about 300 metres and there is traffic ahead and behind you. You should

   a select neutral and use the footbrake to control the speed ☐

   b maintain your speed by using the footbrake all the way down the hill ☐

   c gently brake to give a warning, change down a gear and use the engine to hold back the speed, only applying the footbrake if necessary ☐

22 Is it compulsory to carry a first aid kit in your car in Lithuania?

_____

23 When approaching a zebra crossing in two lanes of slow-moving traffic, what four things should drivers bear in mind, particularly because they are in two lanes of slow-moving traffic?

_____ _____

_____ _____

24 In Norway does traffic on a roundabout have priority over traffic entering?

_____

25 Fig. 5 on Plate K represents the shape of a road traffic sign. Which sign and where would you expect to find it?

_____

_____

26 You are approaching a right-hand bend in your car. Where should you be positioned in the road?

_____

27 While waiting to turn right out of a side road you notice that an approaching driver has flashed the headlights. What should you do?

a Wait because it is not an official signal. ☐

b Wait until you are sure about the other driver's intentions. ☐

c Make progress by proceeding. ☐

d Return the message by flashing your headlights. ☐

28 List four changes to the driving test since its introduction in 1935.

_____

_____

_____

_____

PLATE SECTION

Figure 1

Figure 2

Figure 3

Figure 4

Figure 5

Figure 1

Figure 2

Figure 3

Figure 4

Figure 5

Figure 6

Figure 1

Figure 2

Figure 3

Figure 4

Figure 5

Figure 6

Figure 1

Figure 2

Figure 3

Figure 4

Figure 5

Figure 6

Figure 7

Figure 1

Figure 2

Figure 3

Figure 4

Figure 5

Figure 6

Figure 1

Figure 2

Figure 3

Figure 4

Figure 5

Figure 6

Figure 1

Figure 2

Figure 3

Figure 4

Figure 5

Figure 6

Figure 1

Figure 2

Figure 3

Figure 4

Figure 5 (left)

Figure 6 (above)

Figure 7 (left)

Figure 1

Figure 2

Figure 3

Figure 4

Figure 5

Figure 6

Figure 1

Figure 2

Figure 3

Figure 4

Figure 5

Figure 6

Figure 1

Figure 2

Figure 3

Figure 4

Figure 5

Figure 6

Figure 1

Figure 2

Figure 3

Figure 4

Figure 5 (above)

Figure 6

Figure 7 (left)

Figure 1

Figure 2

Figure 3 (right)

Figure 4

Figure 5

Figure 6

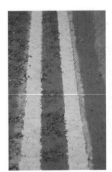

Figure 7

Figure 1

Figure 2

Figure 3

Figure 5

Figure 4

Figure 6

Figure 1 (above)

Figure 2

Figure 3 (right)

Figure 4 (right)

Figure 5 (below)

Figure 6 (above)

29 When taking a B&E category test (to tow a trailer), will the candidate, even though they already hold a full driving licence, have to undergo an eyesight check at the beginning of the driving test?

_____

30 After turning right into a flow of traffic on a major road a driver should

a slow down ☐
b let following traffic overtake ☐
c use the mirrors and adjust the vehicle's speed to the traffic conditions ☐
d slow down and cancel the indicator ☐

31 Engine power output is sometimes advertised in PS rather than brake horsepower. What is PS?

_____

32 Look at Fig. 6 on Plate K. What does this sign mean?

_____

33 What is meant by the term 'brake fade'?

_____

34 When you are being overtaken on an unlit road at night, you should dip your headlights

a well before the vehicle overtakes ☐
b as soon as the vehicle passes ☐
c some time after the vehicle has overtaken ☐
d until the vehicle has overtaken ☐

35 At what age do child cyclist casualties peak?

_____

36 The driver of a vehicle towing a caravan has pulled up along the hard shoulder of a two-lane motorway due to a breakdown. The driver is accompanied by his family. Once on the hard shoulder, what should the driver do first?

_____

37 In 1987 a target was set by the Government for a reduction in road casualties by the year 2000 compared with the average for 1981–85. By how much were the numbers of casualties to be reduced? Was this target met?

_____

38 Traffic signs with a red circle

  a are mostly prohibitive

  b give positive instructions

  c give warnings

  d apply to motor vehicle drivers only

39 You are riding a motorcycle. When can you wait in a yellow painted box junction?

_____

40 After drinking the equivalent of five pints of beer the likelihood of you having an accident is at least 30 times greater than if you had drunk no alcohol. True or false?

_____

Total score for Test 11 _____

SECTION THREE
TEST 12

1 You have to stop quickly in an emergency in a car without ABS. Which of the following are most likely to prevent 'wheel lock'?

a Using the handbrake.

b Selecting neutral.

c Cadence braking.

d Changing up a gear.

2 Look at Fig. 1 on Plate L. The cyclists are riding through a town centre at dusk. Which four precautions should they consider that would make them safer riders (apart from looking where they are going)?

_____

_____

_____

_____

3 Where would you find the 'head shock bearing' on your motorcycle?

_____

4 Two of the most common failure points in the practical driving test for car drivers are incorrect positioning when turning right and incorrect use of the controls when reverse parking. Which one is the more common reason for failure?

_____

5 Look at Fig. 2 on Plate L. What do these road markings mean and where would you see them?

_____

_____

6 You are travelling at 30 mph in fourth gear. You intend emerging to the right at the Stop junction ahead. You should

  a check your mirrors, signal right, brake, change down to second gear and brake to a stop at the line ☐

  b check your mirrors, signal right, gently brake to a stop at the line ☐

  c check your mirrors, signal right, gently brake, select second gear and keep the car moving over the line, looking to see if it is safe ☐

7 What is the maximum fine the court can impose for driving without insurance?

_____

8 What is the maximum term of imprisonment the courts can impose for failing to stop after an accident or failing to report an accident?

_____

9 The driver of a vehicle fitted with automatic transmission is advised to use the left foot on the brake pedal when

   a stopping uphill
   b locking into a lower gear
   c moving along in slow traffic
   d reverse parking in a confined space

10 Name four causes of skidding associated with a motorcyclist's riding errors.

_____

_____

_____

_____

11 What is the blood alcohol legal limit at which you may drive a car in France?

_____

12 What is a segregated track?

_____

13 What colour reflective road studs mark the central reservation on a motorway or dual carriageway?

_____

14 You are about to park the car on the left-hand side of the road. You see that there is no need to signal, and therefore you gently brake and steer into your parking place. Then you should

    a select neutral before the car has stopped and when the car has stopped apply the handbrake and switch off the ignition ☐

    b select neutral as soon as the car has stopped, apply the handbrake and switch off the ignition ☐

    c apply the handbrake as soon as the car has stopped, select neutral and switch off the ignition ☐

15 Look at Fig. 3 on Plate L. If the pedestrian sees this, what does the driver see?

_____

16 Is it compulsory to carry a first aid kit in your car in Ireland?

_____

17 Look at Fig. 4 and Fig. 5 on Plate L. In which picture is the pedestrian acting safely?

_____

18 Is it compulsory to carry a first aid kit in your car in Greece?

_____

19 If one side of a vehicle's dual circuit braking
system fails, the brakes will

  a still work on the front wheels only
  b still work on the rear wheels only
  c still work on one front and one rear wheel
  d stop working completely

20 What is an IDP?

_____

21 You are about to emerge left at the end of the
road. Your vision into the new road, on the
approach to the give way lines, is good. You
should

  a check both ways and, if you can see it is
    safe soon enough, select the appropriate
    gear and emerge, steering left
  b check left and, if you can see it is safe
    soon enough, select the appropriate gear
    and emerge, steering left
  c check right and, if you can see it is safe
    soon enough, select second gear and
    emerge, steering left

22 In Denmark does traffic on a roundabout have
priority over traffic entering?

_____

23 What is a red route?

_____

24 Research shows that it takes two years from passing the driving test before a new driver's accident liability falls. True or false?

_____

25 What percentage of driving test candidates take some professional tuition with a driving school?

a 57%

b 77%

c 97%

26 In most European countries a warning triangle is compulsory. In which two countries is it only recommended?

_____

_____

27 The arm signal necessary to inform an authorised person controlling traffic that you intend to turn left at a road junction is

a an extended left arm with the palm of your hand facing the front windscreen

b an anti-clockwise movement of your right arm

c a clockwise movement of your left arm

d to put your left hand forwards with a finger pointing to the left

28 Look at Fig. 6 on Plate L and identify the sign.

_____

29 European Rules state that if you have been driving a Large Goods Vehicle without a break for four and a half hours, you must take a rest period of what duration?

_____

30 When leaving a mini-roundabout a left turn signal

  a may be unnecessary

  b is always necessary

  c would be inappropriate

  d is a legal requirement

31 At what age do child pedestrian casualties peak?

_____

32 Look at Fig. 7 on Plate L. Where would you find this marker and what does it indicate?

_____

_____

33 You are learning to drive a Large Goods Vehicle (LGV) exceeding the 7.5 tonnage. Can you drive on the motorway during your supervised training?

_____

34 What is the best action to take if you are travelling in dense fog at a speed that you consider safe, and another vehicle begins to follow closely behind?

  a Keep at the same speed and try to reduce any dazzle.

  b Speed up to get away from the vehicle.

  c Slow down and switch on the hazard warning lights.

35 In 1997 the child pedestrian fatality rate per 100,000 head of population in Great Britain was 1.21. Only one European country had a higher fatality rate than this. Which country was it?

---

36 You are driving a very slow-moving vehicle towards a level crossing. What must you do before attempting to cross?

---

37 In a four-stroke engine, the pistons move up and down twice to produce one pulse of power. Order the four strokes below.

Compression ☐
Intake ☐
Exhaust ☐
Power ☐

38 Diamond-shaped traffic signs give directions to

a pedestrians only ☐
b pedestrians and cyclists ☐
c drivers only ☐
d tram drivers only ☐

39 Since 1 January 1988 coaches have had to have speed limiters fitted, set to no more than 100 kph (62 mph). True or false?

---

40 There are eight pieces of information on a vehicle registration document. Name five of them.

_____

_____

_____

_____

_____

Total score for Test 12 _____

52

SECTION THREE
TEST 13

1 When it is necessary to perform an emergency stop the most important thing the driver should do is

   a stop dead
   b brake with the vehicle in a gear
   c react quickly by braking firmly
   d steer out of the skid

2 Look at Fig. 1 on Plate M and imagine that you are the rider of the motorbike in the photograph. Which three things should you be aware of when travelling through slow-moving traffic?

_____

_____

_____

3 When planning a trip through Europe, it is not necessary to take your vehicle registration document. True or false?

_____

4 If you have had a crash for which you could be held at least partly responsible, how much more likely are you to have a similar crash in the next year?

_____

5 Look at Fig. 2 on Plate M. Where would you see this sign and what does it indicate.

_____

_____

6 You are moving off uphill. Which of the following methods would give you the greatest control and put you at least risk of mishap?

a Select first gear, set the gas higher than normal, prepare the handbrake, clutch to the biting point, release the handbrake, check it is safe, signal if necessary, bring the clutch up a fraction to move away. ☐

b Select first gear, set the gas higher than normal, clutch to the biting point, check it is safe, signal if necessary, release the handbrake whilst bringing the clutch up a fraction to move away. ☐

c Select first gear, firmly brake, release the hand-brake, clutch to the biting point, set the gas, check it is safe, signal if necessary, bring the clutch up a fraction to move away. ☐

7 Two attitudes from the list below tend to prevent us from accepting that the risks of driving apply to us as well as to other people. Which are they?

a A high degree of care for our own safety and that of our passengers and other road users. ☐

b A tolerance and consideration for other road users. ☐

c The skilful use of vehicle controls. ☐

d A false sense of personal vulnerability. ☐

e An illusion of control. ☐

8 If you were driving defensively in the following situation what would you have done wrong?
You are driving on an urban dual carriageway. The speed limit is 40 mph and you are travelling at the maximum speed for the road in fifth gear. The weather and road conditions are good and there is not a lot of traffic around. Ahead of you the lights have just changed to red. You check your mirrors and change down to third gear without braking. You then brake to a stop at the lights.

_____

9 When waiting at a red traffic light signal, the driver of a car fitted with automatic transmission should

a select park

b select neutral

c apply the handbrake

d keep the right foot on the footbrake

10 There are two types of braking systems used on motorcycles. What are they?

_____

_____

11 If you were driving defensively in the following situation what would you have done wrong?
It is raining and you are travelling in heavy traffic. You make sure that you have a two-second time gap between you and the vehicle in front, so that you can stop safely if the driver in front stops suddenly.

_____

12 What does SVDD stand for?

_____

13 The biggest influence on fuel consumption, apart from an obvious leak, is driving style. Name three attributes of a driving style that uses more fuel.

_____

_____

_____

14 You are about to overtake a vehicle that is moving slower than you are. Which sequence of actions would be most likely to keep the manoeuvre safe?

a Mirrors – Position – Speed – Look – Mirrors – Signal – Manoeuvre. ☐

b Mirrors – Signal – Manoeuvre. ☐

c Mirrors – Signal – Position – Speed – Look. ☐

15 Look at Fig. 3 on Plate M and identify the sign.

_____

16 It is night and you are driving abroad in Europe. You approach a level crossing and a flashing red light indicates an approaching train. You stop to wait. What must you remember to do when waiting at a level crossing in Europe after dark?

_____

17 Look at Fig. 4 and Fig. 5 on Plate M. Does this paving serve a purpose?

_____

18 You want to drive from Nottingham to Birmingham. What is the most direct route you can take, starting with the A453 at Nottingham and finishing with the A38(M) at Birmingham?

_____

19 The most common cause of spongy brakes is

a a leak on the hydraulic line or the master cylinder

b hydraulic fluid on the brake pads

c worn brake pads

d incorrect shoes

20 What is the name of the phenomenon that can occur when driving at speed in very wet weather?

_____

21 You are driving a car along a road in town. There is traffic following you. Some distance ahead is a parked car with a junction off to the right opposite it. There is no oncoming traffic and plenty of room for you to pass the parked car. Would you give a right-hand signal before moving out?

a Yes. A signal informs other road users of your intentions.

b No. If you pull out early enough, your position acts as a signal informing other road users of your intentions.

c No. There is a side road to the right and your signal might mislead other road users.

22 You want to drive from Northampton to Swansea. What is the most direct route you could take, starting with the A508 from Northampton and finishing with the A483 for Swansea?

_____

23 When did the new law appear which states that if the number of penalty points obtained by a new driver reaches six before two years have lapsed, their licence will be revoked and they would have to pass both the Theory and Practical test again?

_____

24 Taking the most direct route, how many miles is it from Blackburn in Lancashire to Kingston upon Hull?

_____

_____

25 Look at Fig. 6 on Plate M and determine where you would see this sign and what it indicates.

_____

_____

26 The European Union issued a directive in 1991 restricting anyone treated with insulin from driving what classes of vehicles?

_____

_____

27 The arm signal used to inform an authorised
person controlling traffic that you intend to
travel ahead at a road junction is to

  a hold the left hand up with the palm
    facing towards the front windscreen ☐

  b hold the right hand up with the palm
    facing towards the front windscreen ☐

  c point a finger on the left hand directly
    ahead ☐

  d point a finger on the right hand directly
    ahead ☐

28 Taking the most direct route, how many miles is
it from Gloucester to Plymouth?

_____

29 You are the driver of a long Large Goods Vehicle
and are in the process of emerging left from a
minor road on to a major road. Of what two
areas would you be particularly mindful?

_____

_____

30 You are approaching a roundabout. You see a
cyclist signal right. Why would the cyclist keep
to the left?

  a It is a quicker route for the cyclist. ☐
  b The cyclist is going to turn left. ☐
  c The cyclist is vulnerable and taking the
    safest course. ☐
  d The *Highway Code* does not apply to
    cyclists. ☐

31 You must not use hazard warning lights whilst driving except in a particular circumstance. Describe this circumstance.

_____

32 Look at Fig. 7 on Plate M. What do these road markings indicate?

_____

33 Name three organisations that offer first aid training to a professional driver.

_____

_____

_____

34 Visibility can be worse when driving at higher speeds in wet weather because

  a drivers always bunch together

  b headlights will dazzle you more easily

  c of people driving at different speeds

  d more spray is thrown up

35 You are braking on a bend and you start to skid. You feel the rear of the vehicle skid to the right. What two actions should you take?

_____

_____

36 Your Large Goods Vehicle has drifted into deep snow. When trying to free your vehicle you should avoid doing what?

_____

37 You should allow at least a two-second time gap between you and the vehicle in front on roads carrying fast traffic. How much does a two-second time gap give you in distance terms?

_____

38 A positive mandatory traffic sign is:

a blue

b red

c red and blue

d red and white

39 Name four checks that you are recommended to complete before setting out on a motorway journey on your motorcycle.

_____ _____

_____ _____

40 Identify the three faults the driver commits when dealing with a roundabout in the following situation. The driver approaches a roundabout, intending to take the second exit, almost straight ahead. There is no other traffic ahead and on the approach the driver positions in the right-hand lane with a right-hand signal. The driver gives way to the traffic already on the roundabout and joins the round-about in the left-hand lane. Well before the first exit the driver changes the signal to a left-hand signal and exits the roundabout at the second exit.

_____

_____

_____

Total score for Test 13 _____

SECTION THREE
TEST 14

1 When performing an emergency stop the driver should

   a check the mirrors first

   b brake first and then check the mirror

   c brake and de-clutch simultaneously

   d react quickly by braking firmly

2 Look at Fig. 1 on Plate N. What is shown that is illegal?

_____

3 What is likely to happen to a motorcycle if the rider looks down at the front wheel?

_____

4 If you were driving defensively in the following situation what would you have done wrong? You are driving a car in fifth gear at 40 mph, the speed limit for the road. The road ahead slopes very steeply down for about 300 metres and there is traffic ahead and behind you. To maintain your speed you use the footbrake all the way down the hill.

_____

5 Look at Fig. 2 on Plate N and imagine that you are driving a Large Goods Vehicle exceeding 7.5 tonnes along a single carriageway road when you seen this sign. What would your speed limit be in this instance?

_____

6 You are travelling along a national speed limit single carriageway road. There seems to be a problem on the road ahead. The vehicle in front is braking hard. You should

  a start braking and briefly switch on your hazard warning lights to warn following traffic of a hazard ahead

  b start braking and flash your headlights

  c check your mirrors and brake early to warn following traffic, with your brake lights, that you are slowing down

7 What according to _Roadcraft_ is the system of car control?

_____

8 You want to drive from Wolverhampton to Cambridge. What is the most direct route you can take, starting with the A449 at Wolverhampton and finishing with the A1307 at Cambridge?

_____

_____

9 A car fitted with automatic transmission should be left parked on a hill in

a reverse gear

b a forward gear

c park

d neutral

10 You are driving along a normal two-way road with medium traffic flow. Ahead of you are two cyclists riding abreast of each other. Is this allowed?

_____

11 You want to drive from Middlesbrough to Rotherham. What is the most direct route you could take, starting with the A66 at Middlesbrough and finishing with the A629 for Rotherham?

_____

_____

12 In what way is the monotony of driving on the motorway likely to affect your concentration?

_____

_____

13 Taking the most direct route, how many miles is it from Edinburgh to Chester?

_____

14 Hatch markings

    a separate traffic streams

    b are always diagonal stripes with solid
       boundary lines

    c must never be entered in any circumstances

15 Look at Fig. 3 on Plate N. What does this sign
mean?

_____

16 Taking the most direct route, how many miles is
it from Northampton to Swansea?

_____

17 Look at Fig. 4 on Plate N. You're the driver of
the red car emerging to the right. Apart from
checking for traffic and a safe gap, of what must
you be particularly aware as you emerge?

_____

18 If your vehicle fails its M.O.T. test, you can drive
it away from the testing station after failing the
test; you can drive it to have the repairs carried
out; and you can drive to an M.O.T. test
appointment booked in advance. If you are
stopped by the police in any of these
circumstances, can you still be prosecuted?

_____

19 Brake fade will occur when the

    a brakes overheat

    b hydraulic fluid level drops

    c braking linings become worn

    d brakes are not used

20 Vehicles today use coolant in the radiator. A mixture of what makes up coolant?

_____

21 The purpose of box junction markings are to

  a keep junctions clear by preventing traffic from stopping in the path of crossing traffic

  b allow drivers travelling ahead the priority

  c restrict traffic flow and reduce speeds

22 New road safety targets have been set for the year 2010. What percentage has the government set as its target for the reduction in the number of people killed or seriously injured in road accidents compared with the average for 1994–98?

_____

23 When driving abroad you must take your national driving licence with you. True or false?

_____

24 In Sweden does traffic on a roundabout have priority over traffic entering?

_____

25 Look at Fig. 5 on Plate N. What does this tachograph symbol mean?

_____

26 When you turn on your car ignition, warning lights become illuminated. Which warning light normally remains on after you have started the engine?

_____

27 While waiting to make a turn you notice that an approaching driver has flashed the headlights. You should first

a continue to wait in the same position ☐
b make progress by proceeding ☐
c ensure that the other driver's intentions have been understood ☐
d acknowledge the courtesy extended ☐

28 Is it compulsory to carry a first aid kit in your car in Finland?

_____

29 When taking a driving test for B&E, what is the Maximum Authorised Mass (MAM) of your trailer?

_____

30 The main consideration when deciding the speed to travel at, is to

a drive at 30 mph ☐
b drive at the speed limit ☐
c be able to stop within the distance seen to be clear ☐

31 What is the maximum term of imprisonment the courts can impose for causing death by careless driving under the influence of drink or drugs?

_____

32 Look at Fig. 6 on Plate N. What does this sign mean?

_____

33 You are trying to find somewhere to park your vehicle. Driving along a normal two-way road you spot a space on the left-hand side that is free. However when you arrive, you see two painted yellow lines on the kerbstones. What do they mean?

_____

34 What causes extra danger when overtaking in rain?

   a Other vehicles driving slowly.

   b Vehicles wandering across lanes.

   c Increases in vehicle noise.

   d Spray from large vehicles.

35 What colour reflective road studs mark the edge of the main carriageway at lay-bys and slip roads and side roads?

_____

36 If you are driving a large vehicle in wet conditions, what should you aim to do before braking, particularly as far as steering is concerned?

_____

37 What is the blood alcohol legal limit at which you may drive a car in Denmark?

_____

38 How do colour blind drivers recognise red 'Stop' signals at level crossings?

- **a** The light signals will flash up and down. ☐
- **b** The light signals will flash from side to side. ☐
- **c** The light signals will flash from corner to corner. ☐
- **d** The light signals will not flash. ☐

39 Tachographs on Large Goods Vehicles are not required under UK domestic rules. True or false?

_____

40 What is the blood alcohol legal limit at which you may drive a car in Cyprus?

_____

Total score for Test 14 _____

42

SECTION THREE
TEST 15

1 When a driver has to stop suddenly in the wet, the brakes will have their greatest stopping power when

   a the wheels are locked and the tyres are sliding

   b the wheels are nearly, but not quite locked

   c the handbrake is applied

   d driving in the high gears

2 Look at Fig. 1 on Plate O. Which three things should the driver of the overtaking lorry ask himself before attempting to pass the tractor unit?

_____

_____

_____

3 When planning a journey across Europe, what type of organisation could assist you in your route selection and the details of your trip?

_____

4 When may a blue (formerly orange) badge holder not park on yellow lines?

_____

5 Look at Fig. 2 on Plate O. What does this sign denote?

_____

6 When two vehicles approaching from opposite directions both intend to turn right at a crossroads, the decision whether to turn offside (driver's side) to offside or nearside (passenger's side) to nearside depends on

a the road layout, markings and what course the other driver takes ☐

b the drivers avoiding eye contact and sticking to the regulations ☐

c an assumption of driver priorities on the main road ☐

7 What is the maximum fine the court can impose for driving when disqualified?

_____

8 What is the maximum term of imprisonment the courts can impose for dangerous driving?

_____

9 On the approach to a bend the driver of a car fitted with automatic transmission should

a select a lower numbered gear and lock it into position ☐

b slow down by braking and then gently accelerate while steering through the bend ☐

c use kick down to select a lower gear ☐

d use a slowing down arm signal ☐

10 If you customise your Reliant Robin with wide wheels and reduce the headroom, which one of the following should you inform of these modifications?

a Driving Standards Agency.
b DVLA.
c Your insurance company.

11 What is the blood alcohol legal limit at which you may drive a car in the Baltic states?

_____

12 Some traffic lights have an advanced stop line, ahead of the normal stop line. What is this space for?

_____

13 Is it compulsory to carry a first aid kit in your car in Germany?

_____

14 To show your intention to reverse park your car into a parking bay or space at the side of the road you would

a ask your passengers to stop following traffic
b use the mirrors–signal–manoeuvre routine and wait for traffic to clear before showing your reverse lights
c use the mirrors–signal–manoeuvre routine and show your reverse lights as soon as you can

15 Look at Fig. 3 on Plate O. What type of crossing is this?

_____

16 Is it compulsory to carry a first aid kit in your car in France?

_____

17 Look at Fig. 4 and Fig. 5 on Plate O. Which road is more hazardous and how can you tell?

_____

_____

18 Two of the most common failure points in the practical driving test for car drivers are not taking effective observation when emerging from a side road and failure to engage appropriate gears. Which one is the more common reason for failure?

_____

19 When a vehicle has been fitted with an anti-lock braking system this will

 a enable a driver to stop in a shorter distance without skidding ☐

 b allow a driver to brake hard and steer at the same time ☐

 c reduce a driver's safe braking distance ☐

20 Your car is vintage and exempt from Vehicle Excise Duty. What do you have to display?

_____

21 You would consider turning your car round in the road, or making a U-turn to face the opposite direction in a busy high street as

a an acceptable practice providing that you signal your intention to move off ☐

b an acceptable practice providing that you're not hesitant ☐

c a manoeuvre causing inconvenience to others and an unsafe practice ☐

22 New road safety targets for the year 2010 include the objective that there should be a reduction in the number of children killed or seriously injured in road accidents. Compared with the average for 1994–98, what percentage reduction is the Government looking for?

_____

23 A relative is learning to drive and has asked you to take them out for some practice. What are the minimum legal requirements for supervising a learner driver?

_____

_____

24 Taking the most direct route, how many miles is it from Portsmouth to Maidstone?

_____

25 Look at Fig. 6 on Plate 0. What does this sign mean?

_____

26 What is the hard shoulder of a motorway used for?

_____

27 The first thing a driver needs to do when approaching a hazard is to

a reduce speed

b change direction

c check for traffic signs

d check the rear view mirror

28 You want to drive from Porstmouth to Maidstone. What is the most direct route you can take, starting with the A3 from Portsmouth and finishing with the A229 for Maidstone?

_____

_____

29 What should you do if you are towing a trailer and the trailer starts to snake?

_____

30 When driving slowly in urban traffic, the minimum space a driver should leave from the vehicle in front is

a thinking distance

b braking distance

c overall stopping distance

d length of approximately four cars

31 Taking the most direct route, how many miles is it from Wolverhampton to Cambridge?

_____

32 What is the maximum fine the court can impose for seat belt offences?

_____

33 Whilst driving a Large Goods Vehicle, you attempt to overtake another lorry. Due to the uphill gradient you start to lose speed. What should you do?

_____

34 When driving in windy weather, you should

a drive in your usual manner on exposed roads ☐

b anticipate how conditions may affect other road users ☐

c never alter your intended route if this would lengthen your journey ☐

d always overtake smaller or vulnerable vehicles quickly ☐

35 Taking the most direct route, how many miles is it from Gateshead to Nottingham?

_____

36 Under European rules, what is the maximum driving time you are allowed in a two-week period?

_____

37 You want to drive from Blackburn in Lancashire to Kingston upon Hull. What is the most direct route you can take, starting with the A677 at Blackburn and finishing with the A63 for Kingston?

_____

_____

38 Traffic signs giving directions that lead drivers towards a motorway have white information on a

a green background
b blue background
c black background
d red background

39 If you accumulate penalty points from other offences whilst driving other vehicles, your Passenger Carrying Vehicle (PCV) licence will be at risk. True or false?

_____

40 If you were driving defensively in the following situation what would you have done wrong? You are travelling in fourth gear at 30 mph. You intend turning right at the Stop junction ahead, so you check your mirrors, signal right, brake, change down to second gear and brake to a stop at the line. When you can see it is safe you emerge to the right.

_____

Total score for Test 15 _____

Answers and Explanations

1 The correct answer is **c**. Before driving you must ensure that your seating position allows you to reach and use the controls easily.

2 The leading rider is wearing a white helmet. The new *Highway Code*, out in April 2001, recommends motorcyclists could wear a brightly coloured helmet, as well as a white one, to make them more visible.

3 16.

4 One half.

5 Segregated pedal cycle and pedestrian routes.

6 The correct answer is **b**.

7 According to the Official (taken from STATS19) London details on Driving Online, misjudgement of speed and distance at road junctions is the most common cause of accidents. The London figures are fairly representative of the national picture.

8 36 metres (120 feet).

9 The correct answer is **a**. Cadence braking means releasing and reapplying the footbrake. This unlocks the wheels and allows the driver to steer into the direction of the skid, which in this instance is to the left first. If the driver steers too long in the direction of the skid, one is likely to be caused in the opposite direction.

10 A moped up to 125 cc and 11 kw output.

11 70 mph.

12 In turn, spin each wheel and watch. If the wheel is buckled, it will show up where it passes a suspension arm or mudguard stay.

13 Mirrors. Signal. Position. Speed. Look.

14 The correct answer is **c**.

15 Cow dung in the road could make the surface slippery.

16 Motability.

17 The correct answer is **b**. Going down a steep hill, an automatic gearbox system may try to change to a higher gear. The driver is usually able to override this by using the gear selector to remain in a lower gear.

18 For three hours. Prior to 1 April 2000 the Blue Badge Scheme was known as the Orange Badge Scheme.

19 The correct answer is **b**. Cadence braking involves skilful pumping of the brake pedal, releasing it just before the wheels lock and reapplying it for maximum braking effect.

20 The following three conditions are listed in the *DSA Motorcycling Manual.* You must hold a full motorcycle licence; the engine capacity should exceed 125 cc; the trailer must not exceed 1 metre (just over 3 feet) in width. Give yourself one point for each condition correctly identified.

21 The correct answer is **a**.

22 Give yourself one point for each correct answer to a maximum of four points. Ambulance, police car, fire engine, bomb disposal, coastguard.

23 The Traffic Commissioner.

24 Yes.

25 Vehicles can pass either side to reach the same destination.

26 ABS stands for Anti Blockier System. It is a registered trade mark of the German company Bosch. ABS commonly refers to anti-locking braking system.

27 The correct answer is **d**. None of the other responses are flexible enough to fit into the description of driving 'defensively'.

28 50 mg.

29 No. The *Highway Code* says, 'The right-hand lane of a motorway with three or more lanes MUST NOT be used if you are driving a passenger vehicle with a maximum laden weight exceeding 7.5 tonnes constructed or adapted to carry more than eight seated passengers in addition to the driver.'

30 The correct answer is **a**. Thinking distance is also known as reaction time or distance and is usually calculated on the assumption that a vehicle covers one foot per mile an hour of speed. So at 30 mph a vehicle will cover 30 feet in the time it takes for the driver to start braking. This is an average reaction time.

31 True.

32 Stop at the lights.

33 5 metres (16' 5").

34 The correct answer is **a**.

35 Green Card.

36 The 'wave effect' is the movement of the liquid inside the tank of a tanker. Modern tankers are fitted with Baffle plates inside the tank compartments. These are designed to help minimise the movement of the liquid inside the tank and therefore reduce the 'wave effect'.

37 Airway–Breathing–Circulation.

38 The correct answer is **d**. On a one-way street you can position either on the left or the right. No other traffic can turn into the road, so the whole of the width of the road will have a give way road marking.

39 The correct answer is **c**.

40 Driver and Vehicle Licensing Agency in Swansea.

SECTION ONE	TEST 2

1 The correct answer is **a**.

2 The cyclist should be aware of car doors opening suddenly and pedestrians stepping out from in between parked cars. Give yourself one point for each correctly identified risk area.

3 Veer to the right.

4 23 metres.

5 No cycling.

6 The correct answer is **c**. Motorcyclists and cyclists are particularly vulnerable in windy conditions.

7 The overall stopping distance is made up of thinking distance (reaction time) and braking distance.

8 The Blue Badge Scheme. Prior to 1 April 2000 this was known as the Orange Badge Scheme.

9 The correct answer is **c**.

10 The silencer must be marked to certify it is of an approved type.

11 Yes.

12 False. Cyclists are not allowed on the motorways at any time.

13 Doctor's car.

14 The correct answer is **b**. Parked cars can hide children so that you would not see them until the last moment. A slower speed means a shorter stopping distance.

15 A left-hand bend, because the view around a right-hand bend is likely to be better.

16 True.

17 The warning sign will tell you to 'Test your Brakes' after driving through the ford.

18 E111.

19 The correct answer is **a**. Automatic transmissions may try to change to a higher gear when descending hills. Going down a steep hill it may be necessary to keep in a low gear. The driver is usually able to override the transmission by using the gear selector.

20 You should signal right and you should give this signal on the approach to the roundabout. Because you are driving on the right-hand side of the road, the first exit at the roundabout will be to the right. Give yourself two points if you got both parts of the question correct.

21 The correct answer is **c**.

22 The driver.

23 Lamp posts; shop awnings; traffic signs. Give yourself one point for each hazard correctly identified.

24 Driver and Vehicle Licensing Agency (DVLA).

25 Move to the lane to the left.

26 False. Drivers who do not hold a full car (B category) driving licence are not allowed to drive on the motorways.

27 The correct answer is **c**.

28 30 mph. Street lights usually mean that there is a 30 mph speed limit unless there are signs showing another speed limit.

29 Spade; warm clothing; warm drink; emergency food. Give yourself one point for each correct answer.

30 The correct answer is **b**.

31 White.

32 Each half of a zebra crossing, which is divided by a central island, should be treated as a separate crossing. This means that if someone is already crossing from the right-hand side, who has not yet reached the central island, then you may not need to give way to them.

33 The third (right-hand) lane.

34 The correct answer is **b**.

35 No, they are on tracks.

36 30 minutes.

37 10 times greater.

38 The correct answer is **b**.

39 15 months.

40 Yes. Law CUR reg 98, RVLR reg 27 & RTA 1988 sect 42.

| **SECTION ONE** | **TEST 3** |

1 The correct answer is **c**.

2 The two-second rule, which would leave a gap of one metre per mile per hour of speed between the red car and the white van. This is a safe gap so that the driver of the red car could stop safely if the driver of the white van pulled up and stopped suddenly.

3 A full motorbike licence.

4 A GB or EU sticker.

5 The officer is giving a signal to stop.

6 The correct answer is **a**.

7 Yes, parking lights. Law RVLR reg 24. All vehicles MUST display parking lights when parked on a road or a lay-by on a road with a speed limit greater than 30 mph.

8 You must not go beyond the signal in any lane. Law RTA 1988 sect 36 & TSRGD reg 10.

9 The correct answer is **a**.

10 The left-hand lane.

11 Diamond-shaped.

12 Move your passengers to the front of the bus. This is a safety precaution and protects the passengers from risk of injury in the event of the bus being shunted from behind. If it transpires that the bus will be broken down for longer, the passengers should then move on to the embankment.

13 Vehicle Excise Duty.

14 The correct answer is **a**.

15 Test your brakes because they may be soaking wet and need drying out. Give yourself one point if you knew what you should do after driving through a ford and another point if you knew why.

16 Three years old.

17 Yes. The driver should be in the left-hand lane for normal driving.

18 Within seven days.

19 The correct answer is **a**.

20 The correct answer is **b**.

21 A toucan crossing is a pedestrian crossing controlled by lights, which both pedestrians and cyclists can use.

22 Third party only.

23 False. Members of the Sikh religion who wear turbans are exempt.

24 Insurance. You are driving a vehicle that could be unsafe and, in any case, is illegal. There is a higher risk

of accident and so your insurance company would not cover you for any damage incurred.

25 This sign is found on motorways. It means you must leave the motorway at the next exit. You score nothing if you only got part of the question correct; one point if you got both parts correct.

26 True. The majority of countries in Europe require a person to be 18 years old before they can drive a motorcar.

27 The correct answer is **a**.

28 1.6 mm.

29 The correct answer is **a**.

30 The correct answer is **a**.

31 Bottom Dead Centre (BDC).

32 M25.

33 Only when in queues of slow moving traffic and the traffic on your right is moving slower than you are.

34 The correct answer is **a**. The road is only just wide enough for one line of traffic each way. If you position yourself well to the left then you leave more room for vehicles turning into the road you are leaving. Normally the position when turning right should be just to the left of the centre of the road.

35 Tachometer.

36 Long vehicle.

37 Lead replacement petrol (LRP).

38 The correct answer is **d**.

39 You would need to slow your speed down before attempting to overtake the horse; and you would need to ensure that the caravan you were towing was well past the horse before attempting to pull back into the left. Give yourself one point for each issue correctly identified.

40 Catalytic converter.

SECTION ONE	**TEST 4**

1 The correct answer is **b**.

2 There is a pedestrian trying to cross the road behind the lorry. (See legs and feet!)

3 False. Only when a cycle symbol is shown on the bus lane sign can a cyclist use a bus lane.

4 Vehicle Excise Duty.

5 No stopping – clearway.

6 The correct answer is **a**. Give the motorcyclist time and space to make the turn.

7 One year after the date it was issued.

8 1 mm.

9 The correct answer is **a**. If the engine speed is too low you risk stalling and if you drive too fast, you could create a wave and cause water to flood the engine so that it cuts out. It's important to try to strike a balance.

10 120 feet (36 metres).

11 Catalytic converter.

12 You should leave the machine in gear and block the wheel or wedge a wheel against the kerb. Give yourself two points if you got both measures you could take to stop the outfit from rolling away and only one if you only got one. None if you got neither.

13 Hydrogen sulphide gas.

14 The correct answer is **a**. You should never use a warning triangle on a motorway. This is a relatively recent amendment to the *Highway Code*. The faster and busier motorways become the more dangerous it is to be walking along the hard shoulder to place a warning triangle. It is best to wait with any passengers on the embankment until help arrives.

15 The one going uphill is steeper. 15% is steeper than 1:12. 15% is approximately 1:9, which means that for every 9 feet of road, the road rises 1 foot. 1:12 is about 8% and means that for every 12 feet of road, the road drops one foot.

16 Pedestrians; cyclists; horse riders; holders of provisional car licences; holders of provisional motorcycle licences. Give yourself one point for each group identified to a maximum of four points.

17 M25.

18 Advisory.

19 The correct answer is **d**.

20 True.

21 The correct answer is **a**.

22 Briefly use the hazard warning lights.

23 From 1 March 2001 the threshold for the lower rate of Vehicle Excise Duty increased from 1100 cc to 1200 cc.

24 Yes.

25 Blackpool is the seaside town where you are likely to find this sign and it means 'trams only'. You score two points if you got both parts of the question correct; one point if you were only half right.

26 False. The efficiency of modern gearboxes and braking systems makes it unnecessary to change down through each gear in turn. Generally the rule is firstly use the foot brake to reduce your speed, and then select the gear most suitable for that situation and speed.

27 The correct answer is **b**.

28 No.

29 No. Switzerland recommends, but does not enforce, the wearing of rear seat belts.

30 The correct answer is **a**.

31 Department of the Environment, Transport and the Regions.

32 60 mph.

33 No.

34 The correct answer is **a**. If the road you are turning out of is narrow, positioning yourself well over to the left allows room for traffic turning in.

35 85%. Taken from research in March 1999 by Gallup on behalf of Privilege Insurance.

36 April 1999.

37 80 mg.

38 The correct answer is **d**.

39 Your wheels should be pointed to the left-hand side of the hard shoulder. In the event of a vehicle on the carriageway running into the back of your vehicle, it will be shunted to the left and not straight into the left-hand lane.

40 80 mg.

| **SECTION ONE** | **TEST 5** |

1 The correct answer is **d**. The handbrake secures the car. Just braking is risky because in a rear end shunt the driver's foot could come off the footbrake. Selecting neutral is risky because of the possibility of travelling forwards if shunted before the handbrake has been applied.

2 The sign would indicate that there is a risk of grounding.

3 No. Pavement riding isn't allowed.

4 On a left-hand curve.

5 Side winds.

6 **a** is the correct answer. You should be in the left hand lane for normal driving. The middle and right hand lanes are for overtaking only.

7 Bright green/yellow.

8 Contraflow system.

9 The correct answer is **a**.

10 The front brake.

11 'Pass Plus' is a voluntary training scheme created by the Driving Standards Agency for new drivers who would like to improve their basic driving skills and broaden their driving experience.

12 No. All tolls are payable by all British travellers.

13 Institute of Advanced Motorists.

14 **b** is the correct answer. Toucan crossings are for the use of pedestrians and cyclists. There is no flashing amber light.

15 Red and amber together.

16 96 metres.

17 70 mph.

18 No.

19 The correct answer is **c**.

20 No. The signals apply to all traffic using the motorway.

21 **a** is the correct answer. The word 'must' indicates that this is a legal requirement.

22 Yes.

23 Your speed will seem slower than it really is due to driving at a constantly high speed for a number of miles.

24 270 metres, 180 metres, 90 metres.

25 You would see this sign above low bridges. It shows the height restriction on that particular bridge. Give yourself two points if you got both parts of the question correct.

26 National GB plates (or EU plates) must be displayed on the rear of your vehicle. They must also be of an approved size and design.

27 The correct answer is **c**.

28 In service areas. If you feel, however, that service areas are not part of the motorway, and the correct answer is 'nowhere', then you can give yourself one point for this.

29 You should not cross the level crossing until the red light stops flashing. You should ring the signal operator – it might be the barrier has malfunctioned.

30 The correct answer is **a**. To attract your attention a police officer will flash the headlights or the blue lights, or sound the siren or horn. You will then be directed to pull over to the side by pointing and/or a left indicator.

31 0 mg.

32 Red.

33 A hazcem card is a hazard warning plate and you would find this on certain tank vehicles carrying dangerous goods. Give yourself two points if you answered both parts of the question correctly.

34 The correct answer is **c**.

35 80 mg.

36 On a long downhill slope.

37 Royal Society for the Prevention of Accidents.

38 The correct answer is **d**.

39 There is an emergency.

40 53 metres.

| **SECTION TWO** | **TEST 6** |

1 The correct answer is **b**.

2 Yes. On a right-hand bend you should keep to the left of the road to improve your view and to protect you from danger from oncoming traffic.

3 To help reduce accident rates among inexperienced riders.

4 Slow down, because there might be an obstruction around the bend.

5 Cycle route ahead.

6 True.

7 Drop back to maintain the correct separation distance.

8 Slowly, in as high a gear as possible.

9 The correct answer is **a**.

10 The correct answer is **a**. The keywords here are 'very steep', implying that if you moved away in first gear, by the time you brought the clutch fully up you would already be travelling too fast for first gear. On a steep downhill gradient you should move away in second gear to match the speed of the engine with the road speed.

11 The correct answers are **a, b, c**.

12 The motorcyclist should be aware of any vehicle pulling out of the line to overtake the lead vehicle and any vehicle pulling out of a side entrance on the right to turn left. Give yourself two points if you correctly identified both risk areas.

13 The correct answers are **a, d, e**.

14 The correct answer is **b**. There are no other vehicles or pedestrians around so there is no need to signal. Only signalling where necessary encourages you to make effective observations before moving away.

15 Countdown markers on the approach to a concealed level crossing.

16 You shouldn't select neutral until the car has stopped and the handbrake has been applied. You should remain in full control of the vehicle until it is secured.

17 No, the *Highway Code* says you should not cross the road on zig-zag lines. It is not, however, against the law to do so.

18 It is quadrupled.

19 The correct answer is **b**.

20 The *Highway Code* states that you must not carry more than one pillion passenger at any time; they must sit astride the machine on a proper seat; they should keep both feet on the rests provided. Give yourself one point for each point correctly identified, to a maximum of three points.

21 The correct answer is **a**. In a meeting situation like the one described here, the safest option is always to check your mirrors and slow down first. You create time for yourself and can better assess which of you is going to give way. Flashing your headlights can be misinterpreted.

22 Approximately 50 metres.

23 The *Highway Code* states that powered vehicles used by disabled people travel at a maximum speed of 8 mph. On a dual carriageway they must have a flashing amber light, but on other roads you may not have an advance warning.

24 How fast you're going; the gradient on which you're travelling; the weather and the state of the road; the condition of your brakes and tyres; your reaction time. Give yourself one point for each of three factors correctly identified.

25 No motor vehicles.

26 'D' plates are the same as 'L' plates in England. The driver of the vehicle holds a provisional licence and is learning to drive.

27 The correct answer is **a**.

28 The Disability Discrimination Act 1995 outlaws discrimination against disabled people in the areas of goods, facilities and services – this includes insurance.

29 When you are driving to a pre-arranged M.O.T. test appointment.

30 The correct answer is **c**.

31 RAMP stands for Route-Planning and Access Maps Printing. It is operated by The Disabled Motorists' Federation. RAMP can help disabled drivers locate attended pump filling stations and wheelchair accessible cafes.

32 Yes. The solid white lines mean that you should not cross or straddle them. You may cross the line if necessary to overtake a pedal cycle, if it is travelling at 10 mph or less.

33 The air pressure gauge warning of low air pressure in the cylinders.

34 The correct answer is **a**. You should slow down to re-establish a safe gap.

35 Two years old. Children under two years of age do not qualify for a Blue Badge (formerly known as an Orange Badge) because they would not normally be expected to be able to walk independently.

36 Minimum speed limit is 30 mph.

37 Greece. A Blue Badge (formerly known as an Orange Badge) can be used in other European countries but only where there are reciprocal parking arrangements. Norway, Spain, the Republic of Ireland and Gibraltar have no formal reciprocal arrangements; however, parking consideration will be shown to users of the Blue Badge in some situations.

38 The correct answer is **a**.

39 When turning, to avoid mounting the kerb.

40 If a GP is satisfied that there are medical reasons why a person should not wear a seat belt, a certificate can be issued to that effect.

| **SECTION TWO** | **TEST 7** |

1 The correct answer is **c**. In fact, missing out the gears can be safer than changing through the gears one by one. When you use the brakes to slow the car down you are giving a brake light signal to following traffic, informing them that you are slowing down. Also, your footbrake is acting on all four wheels at the same time, whereas if you use the gears to slow down, you are relying on the engine to act as a brake.

2 You should be aware that the motorcyclist could come up on either the nearside or offside of your car to pass you.

3 True. Verboten means 'forbidden'.

4 You should select second gear on a downhill gradient and apply the footbrake. The gradient gives the engine the power it needs to move the car away. You can bring the clutch smoothly and fully up and will find that you are already travelling at a second gear speed.

5 The driver is signalling his intention to move into or turn to the left.

6 **a** and **b** are both correct. **a** is probably safer because positioning well to the left keeps you away from any oncoming traffic. But **b** gives an early view around the bend allowing you to better anticipate danger. Positioning well to the left on a left-hand bend is the advice given in the *Highway Code* and the *Driving Manual*. The police and organisations such as the Institute of Advanced Motorists (IAM) and the Royal Society for the Prevention of Accidents (RoSPA) advise positioning towards the centre of the road.

7 If there is no one around, there is no need to signal. If you always signal to move away, there is a risk that it could become automatic and may mislead other road users if it is not well timed. You should only signal if necessary, to move away.

8 8 mph.

9 The correct answer is **c**.

10 A motorcycle between 75 cc and 125 cc with a power output up to 11 kw.

11 Drive past carefully and do not be distracted by the accident.

12 True.

13 Paramedic.

14 **b** is the correct answer. In the situation described here, there is no priority. Establishing eye contact and looking for clues such as the position of the vehicle, indicators, and the turn of the wheels, help determine who goes first. It is a balance between courtesy and making progress.

15 The sign means 'One-way street'.

16 Orange.

17 You must not overtake the moving motor vehicle nearest the crossing because you cannot guarantee that the motor vehicle is not hiding someone who wants to use the crossing. It is not illegal to overtake a cyclist but you should be careful and make sure that no one is waiting to cross.

18 50 kg.

19 The correct answer is **b**. You should be aware that when the anti-lock brakes are activated, there is a noise which occasionally causes people to release the footbrake as it takes them by surprise. The noise is a normal part of the ABS system.

20 Disqualification.

21 **c** is the correct answer. Only when you've pulled back to increase your separation distance can you see well enough to judge when it is safe to overtake.

22 Woolley Edge J.39–38; Woodall J.31–30; Tibshelf J.29–28; Trowell J.26–25; Donnington Park J.23A; Leicester J.22; Leicester Forest East J.21A–21. Give yourself one point for each service station correctly identified.

23 Kick down on an automatic is a device that provides for quick acceleration when needed.

24 Toucan crossing; puffin crossing; zebra crossing. Give yourself one point for each crossing correctly identified.

25 60 mph.

26 It is an offence to combine cross-ply and radial-ply tyres on the same axle.

27 The correct answer is **a**.

28 £2,500.

29 By pushing down on the front or rear of the vehicle. If it continues to bounce once you've stopped pushing, your shock absorbers may be worn.

30 The correct answer is **d**. Traffic waiting to emerge from the junction opposite at a crossroads has equal priority with the other driver.

31 Alternator.

32 46 metres (150 feet). It is raining and so the overall stopping distance is likely to be doubled.

33 To ensure maximum stability.

34 The correct answer is **d**. The *Highway Code* says that in snowy weather you should watch out for snowploughs, which may throw out snow on either side. You should avoid overtaking them unless the lane you intend to use has been cleared.

35 Two are inlet valves and two are exhaust valves.

36 Keep a tight hold of the steering wheel and decelerate until the vehicle comes to a halt.

37 Glow plugs.

38 The correct answer is **c**.

39 Within 21 days.

40 Transmission.

SECTION TWO	TEST 8

1 The correct answer is **d**. Note that the question does not mention which way the corner bends. Therefore neither **a** nor **b** could be correct.

2 No, it is not an offence to cross or straddle solid white lines if you have to get past an obstruction and the lorry, parked at the side of the road, is causing an obstruction.

3 You might need to increase your tyre pressure to deal with the extra weight the machine is carrying.

4 10%. Taken from *Tomorrow's Roads – Safer for Everyone.* The Government's road safety strategy and casualty reduction targets for 2010.

5 Pre-heating warning light.

6 **c** is the correct answer. A signal should only be used to warn or inform other road users of your intentions to do something – now, not eventually. If you have no intention of pulling out because there is no safe gap, then there is no need to signal.

7 The British Institute of Traffic Education Research.

8 45 mph. Consultation is in process to remove the 45 mph speed restriction for learner drivers and it is more than likely to be scrapped before the end of 2001.

9 The correct answer is **b**.

10 A prop shaft or a chain or belt. Give yourself one point for each item correctly identified.

11 DSA (The Driving Standards Agency).

12 Approximately 100 miles.

13 False. Alcohol is eliminated from the body at a rate approximately equivalent to half a pint of beer each hour. It will take two hours for the body to eliminate one pint of beer.

14 **b** is the correct answer. If, as you turn right from a major road into a minor road, you cause another vehicle to change speed or direction, the gap was not safe and you could have had a crash.

15 If the pedestrian sees a red man the driver would see a green, amber or even red light.

16 True.

17 No, the No Entry words painted on the road indicate it is a one-way street. The van should be positioned on the right-hand side of the road to emerge to the right.

18 The emergency telephone allows easy location by the emergency services.

19 The correct answer is **c**.

20 Power-assisted steering.

21 **c** is the correct answer. When driving you should be constantly scanning the road ahead anticipating where next you will be at risk. A hazard is almost always avoidable if you do this. If you recognise that a hazard is anything that might cause you to change speed or direction, you can take steps to deal with it early and safely.

22 To all lanes.

23 False. A green card is no longer a statutory requirement in the EU; however it is still useful as an internationally recognised proof of insurance cover.

24 Clutch.

25 Park on the pavement.

26 There are 90 metres (100 yards) between each marker. Countdown markers have a blue background with white diagonal stripes. Give yourself one point for each half of the question answered correctly.

27 The correct answer is **c**.

28 On-board diagnostic system (or self-diagnostic system).

29 Amber flashing lights warn of danger ahead.

30 The correct answer is **a**. Offside to offside means driver's door to driver's door, which gives the driver a clear view of the road ahead, making it easier to judge when it is safe to complete the turn.

31 One operates the exhaust valves and one the inlet valves.

32 Yes. The driver is positioned too close to the centre of the road. On right-hand bends you should position well to the left to keep your zone of vision open.

33 You must ensure that your parking brake is applied.

34 The correct answer is **c**.

35 Power. Oil. Water. Electrics. Rubber (tyres and wipers).

36 A diamond shape denoting dangerous cargo.

37 Catalytic converter.

38 The correct answer is **c**.
39 The Public Service Vehicle Operator's Licence.
40 Parliament.

SECTION TWO	TEST 9

1 The correct answer is **a**.
2 No. This manoeuvre is not illegal. However, it is not recommended to cut right-hand corners, as it could be a very dangerous manoeuvre, especially where visibility into the new road is restricted.
3 It is the last check over your shoulder, into your blind spot, before joining the main carriageway.
4 You did not check left before emerging. This is a common cause of accidents where oncoming traffic is on your side of the road as you emerge because they have an obstruction on their side of the road. You must take effective observation before emerging which means looking both ways and deciding it is safe, before crossing the give way line.
5 There might be a fault in the braking system.
6 **a** is the correct answer. A vehicle is at its most stable under constant acceleration around a bend. Therefore, you should slow down first, match the gear to the speed and gently accelerate around the bend.
7 Hazard warning lights must only be used for this purpose on a dual carriageway or motorway.
8 Millar certificate.
9 The correct answer is **c**. Although most automatics have a cut-out switch that prevents you from starting in gear, you should always check that the selector is in the park or neutral position and the handbrake is fully applied before starting the engine.
10 You must be aware of crosswinds, rain, fog, ice, snow, and the sun which, if low in the sky, can be dazzling. Give yourself one point for each problem correctly identified to a maximum of three.

11 Yes.

12 Do not go beyond the red light in that lane.

13 Sedgemoor, M5, Junction 21–22.

14 **c** is the correct answer.

15 At the end of a dual carriageway; at the end of a one-way system. Give yourself two points if you correctly identified both instances; one point if you only got one.

16 0.3 metres.

17 No. The blue sign in the middle of the picture is telling you that you can 'pass either side to reach the same destination'.

18 Stop and have a short sleep (up to 15 minutes) or have a drink, such as two cups of strong coffee. (There is recent research which suggests that coffee is not as effective as was once thought at counteracting sleepiness.) Give yourself one point for each measure correctly identified.

19 The correct answer is **b**.

20 Driving too slowly for the road and traffic conditions is the more common reason for failure. This is to do with, for example, failing to keep up with the flow of traffic. So if the speed limit is 40 mph and the candidate is driving at just over 30 mph and holding up the traffic, then an error will be marked here. Hesitation, however, is usually related to emerging at junctions and an error may be recorded because the candidate has failed to take sufficient advantage of safe gaps in which to emerge.

21 **b** is the correct answer.

22 20.5 metres (67 feet). New number plates are about to be introduced (2001). The font size on these is 64 mm and the distance from which you must be able to read the number plate is 20 metres. The arrangement of the letters and numbers is also changing. The first two letters identify the place of issue, followed by two numbers and then three letters.

23 May 1999.

24 No. You should never use warning triangles on motorways.

25 The symbol means break/rest period and is a tachograph symbol.

26 The correct answer is **b**. The driver need wait only until the pedestrians have reached the central refuge. The crossing is treated as two separate crossings. You should give way to pedestrians who are waiting to cross the road at a zebra crossing, even if they have not got one foot on the crossing, if it is safe to do so. Therefore **c** is incorrect.

27 The correct answer is **a**.

28 12 points over a three year period.

29 Pedestrians/children crossing between the parked cars; car doors opening; cars pulling out; animals that cannot be seen above the stationary vehicles. Give yourself one point for each hazard correctly identified.

30 The correct answer is **d**.

31 10 years.

32 No, it's a one-way street.

33 The driver's employer.

34 The correct answer is **a**.

35 Distributor.

36 1 mm.

37 The catalyst.

38 At the Driving Standards Agency's training establishment at Cardington in Bedfordshire.

39 Another name for a gearbox with high and low ratios.

40 Clutch.

| **SECTION TWO** | **TEST 10** |

1 The correct answer is **b**. If the handbrake should fail the car will roll down the hill. If the wheels are facing to the right then the car will roll into the kerb, which may stop the car from rolling any further.

2 The car is parked outside a school and the yellow zig-zag lines mean that it should not be parked there.

3 Yes. EU licences are valid in the UK.

4 You should only flash your headlights to let another road user know you are there. By slowing down and steering into a gap on the left you have informed the approaching driver that you are giving way without needing to flash your headlights as well.

5 A protection or side marker. This is often seen on the rear of large vehicles.

6 The correct answer is **b**.

7 'S' stands for signal and, in this instance, the signal you would be using would be the brake lights. Give yourself one point for each part of the question correctly identified.

8 You must not use the horn when stationary on the road or when driving in a built up area between 11.30 pm and 7.00 am. The exception to both of these is when another vehicle poses a danger. Give yourself one point for each part of the question correctly identified.

9 The correct answer is **d**.

10 A cyclist in foggy conditions should ensure that the lights on the front and rear of their bike are working and that they are wearing brightly coloured reflective clothing. Give yourself two points, one for each part of the question correctly answered.

11 You must stop, by law, at a stop sign. Laws RTA 1988 sect 36 & TSRGD regs 10 & 16.

12 You could expect the cyclist to either move to the right or turn right ahead.

13 No, but unsafe. If possible you should reverse in and drive out.

14 The correct answer is **c**. The sequence of lights at a puffin crossing is: Red – Red and Amber – Green – Amber – Red. There is no need for a flashing amber phase because the lights are held on red as long as someone is on the crossing.

15 A temporary road works speed limit sign is mandatory.

16 100 metres (328 feet).

17 You 'should'. If they have one foot on the crossing, you 'must' by law give way.

18 You must have held a full car licence for at least three years and be at least 21 years of age.

19 The correct answer is **a**.

20 The same as everybody else – right-hand side.

21 **c** is the correct answer.

22 When a police officer asks for it; when you are taxing your vehicle; when you have been involved in an accident. Give yourself two points if you correctly identified two instances when you must show your insurance certificate.

23 Because it releases no lead into the atmosphere.

24 The seller.

25 You would reduce speed and select the appropriate gear to descend the downhill gradient.

26 No. With street lighting, the speed limit is normally 30 mph. If the speed limit is greater than 30 mph, you must leave parking lights on.

27 The correct answer is **c**.

28 A nil licence.

29 A = Airway   B = Breathing   C = Circulation.

30 The correct answer is **b**.

31 Six points within two years of the date of passing their driving test. Give yourself two points if you correctly answered both parts of the question.

32 No. Outside of the waiting limit, Monday to Saturday 8 am–6 pm, there is no waiting allowed.

33 In the vehicle manufacturer's handbook.

34 The correct answer is **a**. The headlights will dazzle an oncoming driver earlier on a left-hand bend than on a right-hand bend.

35 For every faulty tyre there is fixed fine up to £2,500, discretionary disqualification, and a driving licence endorsement.

36 After passing a motorcyclist you should check the left door mirror to ensure that it is safe to move back in because motorcyclists are very vulnerable to crosswinds.

37 False. The eyesight test on the driving techniques part of the driving instructor's qualifying examination is stricter than on the learner driver's test. You must be able to read a number plate from a distance of 27.5 metres. New number plates are being introduced (2001) with a smaller font size of 64 mm. The distance from which you must be able to read a new-size number plate is 27 metres.

38 The correct answer is **a**.

39 Driving three abreast reduces your escape options in the event of an emergency.

40 £1,000.

| **SECTION THREE** | **TEST 11** |

1 The correct answer is **a**.

2 The motorcyclist should not have parked there because parking on double yellow lines is illegal and because it is dangerous to be parked so close to the bend. Give yourself one point for each reason you correctly identified.

3 She is signalling her intentions to either move to the left or turn left.

4 Twice as likely. If you do have an accident, statistics indicate that your chances of having a similar one in the next three years are doubled. If you were partly responsible for the accident, you are four times more likely to be involved in a similar one within the next year. This is because your behaviour will remain unchanged if you seriously believe you did not help to cause the accident. Taken from BSM's *Pass your Driving Theory Test*.

5 With-flow pedal cycle lane.

6 **b** is the correct answer. Generally speaking, if you can see that you will have to stop, you should brake to a stop in the gear you are in. This is safer than changing down because you keep both hands on the wheel and concentrate on the road ahead. 'Brakes to slow, gears to go.'

7 Incorrect use of the controls when reversing.

8 £1,000.

9 The correct answer is **a**. When manoeuvring in an automatic vehicle, it is safe to do so with one foot on each pedal. In normal driving, however, it is safer to use the right foot only for the accelerator and the brake pedals.

10 Green. Cycle tracks on opposite sides of the road may be linked by crossings controlled by lights. Cyclists may ride across on these but only when the green cycle symbol is showing.

11 Six months (12 months in Scotland).

12 To see and be seen. Give yourself two points if you got both considerations.

13 Red.

14 **a** is the correct answer. A larger gap in front of you gives you and the vehicle behind more time to stop in an emergency. A four-second time gap is recommended where the roads are wet.

15 The sign means road narrows on both sides.

16 50 mg.

17 Parking on double yellow lines. Parking half on the pavement. And, if it were dark, parking against the flow of traffic.

18 No.

19 The correct answer is **a**.

20 On an adverse camber the road slopes up towards the outer edge of the road, as opposed to an ordinary camber, where the road slopes up towards the centre of the road, allowing for drainage into the gutters.

21 **c** is the correct answer. On a long downhill slope
   constant use of the footbrake to slow the car down
   could result in the brakes overheating. A lower gear
   holds the car back and then the footbrake can just be
   applied occasionally.

22 Yes.

23 Drivers must avoid obstructing the crossing; they
   should not move off if they cannot see the opposite
   side of the crossing; they must not overtake the
   moving motor vehicle closest to the crossing; nor
   must they overtake the lead vehicle that has stopped
   to give way. Give yourself one point for each
   consideration correctly identified, up to a maximum
   of four points.

24 Yes.

25 A stop sign. You would expect to find it at the end of
   a road where visibility is perhaps restricted and where
   you must stop before giving way.

26 You should keep to the left to improve your vision
   around the bend and keep away from the danger of
   oncoming traffic.

27 The correct answer is **b**. It's necessary to make sure
   that the signal is meant for you and that you are being
   invited to emerge; it is also necessary to make sure
   that it is safe to emerge. The driver approaching could
   be flashing the headlights at a pedestrian or cyclist or
   another driver – be certain that this is not the case
   before acting on somebody else's signal.

28 Give yourself one point for each correct answer to a
   maximum of four points.
   Removal of arm signals
   Addition of a reverse parking exercise
   A separate Theory Test
   Changes to the length of the practical driving test
   Three out of four possible manoeuvres
   Optional emergency stop exercise
   15 driver errors = fail.

29 Yes.

30 The correct answer is **c**. It is dangerous to emerge and cause another vehicle to change speed or position because of you. If you check the mirrors as soon as you have emerged, you can adjust your speed accordingly to avoid causing these problems.

31 Pferdestarke. This is German for horsepower. 1 bhp (brake horsepower) is equivalent to 1.0139 PS – so almost the same.

32 With-flow bus and cycle lane. The times of operation are shown on the plate underneath.

33 A reduction of braking effectiveness after excessive use, for example continually using the brake whilst going down a long decline. If used too much, the brakes get hot and hot brakes are not as efficient as cold ones.

34 The correct answer is **b**. If you dip the headlights too late you risk dazzling the driver who has just overtaken.

35 At about the age of 14. Taken from *Tomorrow's Roads – Safer for Everyone*. The Government's road safety strategy and casualty reduction targets for 2010.

36 The driver should ensure that all passengers leave the vehicle from the left and move as far away from the carriageway as possible.

37 By one third. The target was more than achieved. Road deaths have fallen by 39% and serious injuries by 45% making Britain one of the safest countries in Europe and the world. However, there has not been any such steep decline in the number of accidents, nor in the number of slight injuries, although improvements in vehicle design have helped to reduce the severity of injuries to car occupants. Taken from *Tomorrow's Roads – Safer for Everyone*. The Government's road safety strategy and casualty reduction targets for 2010. Give yourself two points if you correctly answered both parts of the question.

38 The correct answer is **a**.

39 When you are turning right and are prevented from doing so by oncoming traffic.

40 True. Just one drink is enough to impair your driving performance. Having twice the legal limit of alcohol in your blood makes you at least 30 times more likely to have an accident than if you had not had an alcoholic drink at all.

SECTION THREE	**TEST 12**

1 The correct answer is **c**.

2 The cyclists should consider wearing cycle helmets; using lights on the front and rear of their bikes; wearing reflective clothing; and not riding two abreast. Give yourself one point for each precaution the cyclists could take, that you correctly identified, up to a maximum of four.

3 A head shock bearing is part of the steering and suspension system at the front of the bike.

4 Incorrect use of the controls when reverse parking.

5 The road markings mean Give Way to traffic on the major road and you would find them at the junction between a minor and a major road. Give yourself two points if you correctly answered both parts of the question.

6 **b** is the correct answer. At a Stop junction, you must stop, so there is no need to select second gear on the approach. Brake to a stop in fourth gear and then select first to emerge when it is safe. Keeping both hands on the wheel and your eyes and mind fully on the road ahead is less risky than taking one hand off the wheel to change down a gear unnecessarily.

7 £5,000.

8 6 months.

9 The correct answer is **d**.

10 Heavy or uncoordinated braking; excessive acceleration; swerving suddenly to change direction; leaning over too far when cornering. Give yourself one point for each rider error correctly identified to a maximum of four points.

11 50 mg.

12 A segregated track is intended for joint use by pedestrians and cyclists. A pedestrian must keep to the side of the segregated track intended for cyclists.

13 Amber.

14 **c** is the correct answer. Selecting neutral before applying the handbrake is potentially dangerous. If another vehicle shunted you from behind you are at risk of travelling forwards because there is nothing holding the car back. Applying the handbrake first and then selecting neutral is the safest way to secure the car.

15 The driver sees a red light.

16 No.

17 In both. It is generally safest to walk facing the oncoming traffic where there are no footpaths. However, on a blind right-hand bend the safest thing to do is to position yourself where you can see and be seen – on the left-hand side.

18 Yes.

19 The correct answer is **c**. With a dual hydraulic braking system the brakes are diagonally linked so that if one side fails, the brakes will still operate on the diagonally opposite wheels.

20 International Driving Permit.

21 **a** is the correct answer. Emerging left and only checking to the right is a common cause of accidents. You must check both ways in order to judge that it is safe to emerge.

22 Yes.

23 Red routes are stopping/parking controls used instead of yellow lines in some parts of large towns and cities across the UK.

24 True. 'Newly qualified drivers, the majority of whom are also young drivers, are at particularly high risk after passing the driving test. As many as one in five new drivers has an accident in the first year and whereas 17–21-year-olds represent only about 7 per

cent of all licence holders, they make up 13 per cent of drivers involved in injury accidents.' Taken from *Road Safety Research Series No.2. Novice Driver's Safety.* Published by the Department of the Environment, Transport and the Regions (DETR).

25 The correct answer is **c**. This figure is based on findings from *The Cohort Study*, which involved approximately 29,500 driving test candidates – all those who took a driving test on two days in November 1988 and two days in July 1989. Taken from *Road Safety Research Series No.2. Novice Driver's Safety.* Published by the Department of the Environment, Transport and the Regions (DETR).

26 Spain and the UK.

27 The correct answer is **a**.

28 Give priority to vehicles from the opposite direction.

29 45 minutes.

30 The correct answer is **a**.

31 At about the age of 12. Taken from *Tomorrow's Roads – Safer for Everyone.* The Government's road safety strategy and casualty reduction targets for 2010.

32 You would find this marker along the edge of the motorway hard shoulder. Markers like this indicate the direction to the nearest emergency telephone, which connects directly to the police. Give yourself one point for each part of the question correctly answered.

33 Yes.

34 The correct answer is **a**.

35 Ireland had a child pedestrian fatality rate per 100,000 head of population of 1.31 in 1997. Taken from *Tomorrow's Roads – Safer for Everyone.* The Government's road safety strategy and casualty reduction targets for 2010.

36 You must obey any sign instructing you to use the telephone to obtain permission to cross the level crossing.

37 Intake   Compression   Power   Exhaust.

38 The correct answer is **d**.

39 True.

40 Give yourself one point for each correct answer up to a maximum of five points.

Date of first registration

Registration number

Previous keeper

Registered keeper

Make of vehicle

Engine size and chassis number

Year of manufacture

Colour.

| **SECTION THREE** | **TEST 13** |

1 The correct answer is **c**.

2 You should be aware of vehicles suddenly changing lanes or direction; vehicles emerging suddenly from junctions that cannot be seen clearly due to the volume of traffic; pedestrians crossing the road between stationary traffic. Give yourself one point for each problem correctly identified.

3 False. A vehicle registration document must be carried when driving a UK-registered vehicle abroad. Taken from *Motoring in Europe – The essential handbook for the independent motorist abroad* by RAC Motoring Services Ltd.

4 Four times as likely.

5 This sign would be displayed in the front and rear window of a school bus. It warns of children in and around the bus if it is parked.

6 a is more correct than **b**. **c** is wrong. **b** is not wrong. However, **a** gives you the greatest degree of control because at the point when the car starts moving, you have both hands on the wheel.

7 The correct answers are **d** and **e**. A false sense of personal vulnerability and an illusion of control.

8 Change down to third gear without braking. You

shouldn't use the gears to slow the car down in normal driving. The brakes are safer and signal to following traffic that you are changing speed.

9 The correct answer is **c**. Applying the handbrake when the vehicle is stationary is more important in an automatic than in a manual car. In an automatic car, unless the gear selector is in park or neutral the car will move forwards when the accelerator is pressed.

10 Mechanically operated and hydraulically operated. Give yourself two points if you got both parts correct.

11 It is raining, so the gap you leave should be at least four seconds, not two.

12 Speed Violation Detection Deterrent. This is some of the latest video camera technology. It accurately detects speeding offences by reading number plates. ACPO (Association of Chief Police Officers) approved of the system and supported its application for Home Office Type Approval (HOTA). Two Police Forces, Kent and Leicestershire, championed the trials testing on the M1 and M20 road works between 1993 and 1995.

13 Heavy acceleration; harsh braking; changing gear frequently. Give yourself one point for each attribute correctly identified.

14 **a** is the correct answer. Before overtaking, considering your position – not so close that you cannot see past the vehicle you want to overtake – and your speed – a lower gear gives you more acceleration – best prepare you for the manoeuvre.

15 No Entry.

16 Switch off the headlights.

17 Yes, tactile paving lets blind people feel where it is safe to cross the road.

18 A453, M1, A42, M42, M6, A38(M).

19 The correct answer is **a**.

20 Aquaplaning. This is a build up of water between the tyres and the road surface. As a result, the vehicle slides forward on a thin film of water as your tyres lose contact with the road.

21 **c** is the correct answer. It is never necessary to automatically give a signal. Check your mirrors and the road ahead first before deciding whether, when and how to signal. Your position can indicate your intentions, as can your speed.

22 A508, A45, A43, M1, M6, M42, M5, M4, A483.

23 1 June 1997.

24 113 miles. Score a point for an estimate between 100 and 120. If you guessed 113 miles, score two points.

25 You find this sign on the motorway and it indicates a crawler lane ahead to allow slow-moving vehicles to keep to the left on uphill gradients.

26 Any vehicle over 3.5 tonnes and minibuses with more than eight passenger seats.

27 The correct answer is **a**.

28 146 miles. Score a point for an estimate between 135 and 155 miles. If you guessed 146 miles, score two points.

29 You would have to ensure that traffic is clear from both directions – you will be taking up a large proportion of the opposite lane; and you would need to be aware of pedestrians on the left-hand corner of the pavement during the manoeuvre. Give yourself one point for each part of the question you answered correctly.

30 The correct answer is **c**.

31 Briefly on a motorway or dual carriageway where you need to warn drivers behind you of a hazard ahead.

32 No waiting at any time.

33 St John Ambulance Association and Brigade; St Andrew Ambulance Association; The British Red Cross. Give yourself one point for each organisation you thought of.

34 The correct answer is **d**.

35 Ease off the brake; steer smoothly to the right.

36 Continually revving in a low gear.

37 One metre per mile per hour. So, at 40 mph a two-second time gap would give you a distance of 40 metres between you and the vehicle in front.

38 The correct answer is **a**.

39 You should check you have enough fuel for the journey; the tyres are correctly inflated; the lights and indicators are in working order; and any load is securely fastened to your machine. Give yourself one point for each check correctly identified.

40 Give yourself one point for each fault identified (three points in total). The driver should have approached in the left-hand lane. The driver should not have indicated on the approach. The driver should have indicated left on passing the first exit.

SECTION THREE	TEST 14

1 The correct answer is **d**.

2 The lorry has parked on the zig-zag lines of a zebra crossing.

3 Looking down at the front wheel can severely upset the rider's balance.

4 You should have selected a lower gear and used the engine to hold your speed back, only applying the footbrake as necessary.

5 National speed limit applies, which is 40 mph on a single carriageway road for LGVs exceeding 7.5 tonnes.

6 **c** is the correct answer. Hazard warning lights may only be used on motorways and dual carriageways to warn following traffic of a hazard ahead.

7 Information. Position. Speed. Gear. Acceleration.

8 A449, M54, M6, A14, A1307.

9 The correct answer is **c**.

10 Yes, as long as they are aware of traffic conditions and return to single file if and when necessary, for example, if the road narrows.

11 A66, A19, A168, A1(M), A1, M1, A629.

12 You could start to feel tired and sleepy.

13 240 miles. Score a point for an estimate between 220 and 260. If you guessed 240 miles, score two points.

14 **a** is the correct answer. Hatch markings are diagonal stripes with either solid or broken boundary lines which is why **b** is wrong.

15 Level crossing with gate or barrier ahead.

16 200 miles. Score a point for an estimate between 185 and 215. If you guessed 200 miles, score two points.

17 The zebra crossing.

18 Yes, you can still be prosecuted if your car is not roadworthy under the various regulations governing its construction and use. You won't, however, be prosecuted for driving without a current M.O.T. test certificate.

19 The correct answer is **a**.

20 Water and anti-freeze.

21 **a** is the correct answer. You should make sure your exit from the box junction is clear before entering. If it is not clear you should wait behind the line.

22 40%. Taken from *Tomorrow's Roads – Safer for Everyone*. The Government's road safety strategy and casualty reduction targets for 2010.

23 True.

24 Yes.

25 Other work or On Duty and available for work.

26 The handbrake warning light.

27 The correct answer is **c**.

28 No.

29 One tonne.

30 The correct answer is **c**.

31 10 years.

32 No pedestrians.

33 No loading at anytime.

34 The correct answer is **d**.

35 Green.

36 Before braking in wet conditions you should try to ensure that your vehicle is travelling in a straight line.

37 50 mg.

38 The correct answer is **b**.

39 True. Until EU regulations made it compulsory to have tachographs drivers in the UK were not forced to use them.

40 90 mg.

| **SECTION THREE** | **TEST 15** |

1 The correct answer is **b**.

2 Is it necessary? Is it safe? Is it legal? If the answer to any one of these questions is 'No', then the overtaking manoeuvre probably shouldn't be carried out. Give yourself one point for each issue correctly identified.

3 All major motoring organisations such as the RAC.

4 When there is a ban on loading or unloading.

5 Ring Road.

6 **a** is the correct answer. Where there are no road markings and the road layout is square, not staggered, turning offside to offside is often safer because you have a clear view of the road ahead and can judge a safe gap in the traffic.

7 £5,000.

8 Two years.

9 The correct answer is **b**.

10 The correct answer is **c**. You should inform your insurance company.

11 0 mg.

12 It allows cyclists to move away from the traffic lights just ahead of the normal traffic flow.

13 No.

14 **c** is the correct answer. By showing your reverse lights as soon as you can you make your intentions clear to following drivers.

15 Toucan.

16 No.

17 Fig. 4 is more hazardous. This is obvious because of the hazard road markings down the middle of the road and the crossroad junction.

18 Not taking effective observation when emerging from a side road is the more common reason for failure.

19 The correct answer is **b**.

20 A nil licence.

21 **c** is the correct answer. The safest thing to do is to find a quiet side road to turn around in.

22 50% Taken from *Tomorrow's Roads – Safer for Everyone*. The Government's road safety strategy and casualty reduction targets for 2010.

23 The supervisor of a learner driver must hold a full EC/EEA licence for that type of vehicle and have held one for at least three years and they must be at least 21 years old.

24 100 miles. Score a point for an estimate between 90 and 110. If you guessed 100 miles, score two points.

25 Two-way traffic crossing a one-way street.

26 Emergencies only.

27 The correct answer is **d**.

28 A3, M275, A27, A29, A264, (or A280, A24) A24, A264, M23, M25, M26, M20, A229.

29 Ease off the accelerator and reduce speed gently.

30 The correct answer is **a**. Ideally, in any situation, you would leave at least the overall stopping distance. This is not always safe and practical, particularly in heavy, slow-moving traffic. In such a situation, the thinking distance is the bare minimum.

31 113 miles. Score a point for an estimate between 100 and 120. If you guessed 113 miles, score two points.

32 £1,000.

33 Ease off the accelerator and drop back behind the vehicle you are trying to overtake.

34 The correct answer is **b**.

35 158 miles. Score a point for an estimate between 145 and 170. If you guessed 158 miles, score two points.

36 90 hours.

37 A677, A677(M), M65, A6177, A56, M66, M62, A63.

38 The correct answer is **b**.

39 True.

40 There is no need to select second gear if you know you have to stop the car.

TEST 16

Test 16 is an actual IQ test. The other tests are quizzes, designed so that you can test your knowledge, either on your own or in groups. When you total up the number of points you gain for a test, you get an idea of how well you did, matched against your personal expectations. If you consider yourself to be very knowledgeable about driving-related issues, you would be satisfied with a high score. On the other hand, if you feel you know very little about driving and are not particularly interested in the subject, you would not be surprised if you scored quite low.

Test 16 is different because this test has been posted on the Internet and the data collected from the completed tests has been collated so that you can compare your score with the sample from the Internet. You can read more about how this process worked and what the data has revealed in the next few pages.

If you have completed the previous 15 tests, then you have already answered the 43 IQ questions that form Test 16. You will need to refer back to these questions so that you can record the answers you gave in the table below.

How to complete the table
The column headed 'Reference' is the test and question number reference. So for the first answer you need to look at Test One, question 6 and record the response you gave in the next column, headed

'Your answer'. The next column, headed 'Answer', indicates the correct response to the question. In the next column, headed 'Score', you should record '0' if you answered incorrectly and '1' if you answered correctly. There is space to record your responses to the 43 questions. Finally, total up all the 1s and make a note of your total score.

If you scored between 0 and 26, you have gained a copper award.

If you scored 27 or 28, you have gained a bronze award.

If you scored 29 or 30, you have gained a silver award.

If you scored between 31 and 33, you have gained a gold award.

If you scored between 34 and 43, you fall into the top 20% and have gained a platinum award.

In order to validate an IQ test, the questions that you have answered need to have been answered by a sample of people before you. This allows the test results of the sample to be analysed to produce a range of average scores so that you can have an accurate interpretation of how well you did in comparison with the sample group.

Reference	Your answer	Answer	Score	Reference	Your answer	Answer	Score
T 1.6		B		T 8.21		C	
T 1.14		C		T 9.6		A	
T 1.21		A		T 9.14		C	
T 2.6		C		T 9.21		B	
T 2.14		B		T 10.6		B	
T 2.21		C		T 10.14		C	
T 3.6		A		T 10.21		C	
T 3.14		A		T 11.6		B	
T 3.20		B		T 11.14		A	
T 4.6		A		T 11.21		C	
T 4.14		A		T 12.6		B	
T 4.21		A		T 12.14		C	
T 5.6		A		T 12.21		A	
T 5.14		B		T 13.14		A	
T 5.21		A		T 13.21		C	
T 6.10		A		T 14.6		C	
T 6.14		B		T 14.14		A	
T 6.21		A		T 14.21		A	
T 7.14		B		T 15.6		A	
T 7.21		C		T 15.14		C	
T 8.6		C		T 15.21		C	
T 8.14		B					
				Total score:			

Between October 2000 and the end of December 2000, the 43 questions you have just scored yourself on were posted on the Internet with links from websites run by BSM, RAC, Driving and Virgin Publishing. A total of 2,760 people completed the IQ test during this period and the test results can be seen in the following graph.

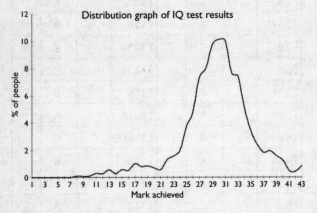

Distribution graph of IQ test results

The following information shows who scored what and illustrates the data used for the above distribution graph.

0%	scored 1–5	39.96%	scored 26–30
0.27%	scored 6–10	33.69%	scored 31–35
2.02%	scored 11–15	9.07%	scored 36–40
3.93%	scored 16–20	1.81%	scored 41–43
9.25%	scored 21–25		

An IQ (intelligence quotient) test is designed to measure general aptitude for learning. The French psychologist Alfred Binet developed the first successful intelligence tests. The revision of Binet's scales adopts the intelligence quotient (IQ) as an index of mental development. The IQ expresses intelligence as a ratio of mental age to chronological age.

From this description you can see that *Test Your Driving IQ* applies the term IQ loosely. The fact that 2,760 people completed the questions and gave an index against which to measure your performance when answering the same questions is the only justification for calling it an IQ test. It is merely interesting to see how your level of driving knowledge matches against a sample of so many people.

Furthermore, there is no suggestion that from these statistics anything can be deduced regarding the extent to which what you know affects how you drive: if you scored well you are not necessarily a good driver and if you scored poorly nor are you necessarily a bad driver. The reason no correlation can be made between knowledge and driving in a test like this is because your driving has not been assessed. Knowledge is, of course, important, but far more crucial is how that knowledge is applied when you are behind the wheel of a car.

The questionnaire posted on the Internet asked six questions of the respondents before allowing them to go on and complete the test. The six questions were:

1 Are you male or female?
2 How old are you?
3 How old were you when you passed the driving test?
4 For how many years have you been driving?
5 What is your weekly average mileage?
6 How many accidents have you had in the last three years?

The graphs on the following pages illustrate the results of the data collected from these questions. It is beyond the scope of this book to attempt to analyse the data or draw any conclusions from it. Much more detailed research and analysis would need to be undertaken to establish whether there is any correlation between what you know and what you do. And remember, whatever the following charts might suggest to you, they are limited to driving knowledge.

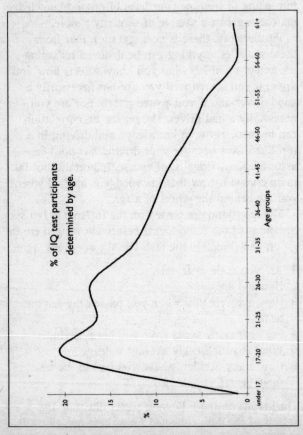

% of IQ test participants determined by age.

%

under 17 · 17-20 · 21-25 · 26-30 · 31-35 · 36-40 · 41-45 · 46-50 · 51-55 · 56-60 · 61+

Age groups

The first chart (bottom left) shows how old the people in the sample are. It also probably indicates the age of people who surf the net.

The next chart (below) shows what the men scored and what the women scored. Although there is no really obvious difference between the two groups, slightly more men achieved higher results than women ... and yet women have fewer road accidents than men.

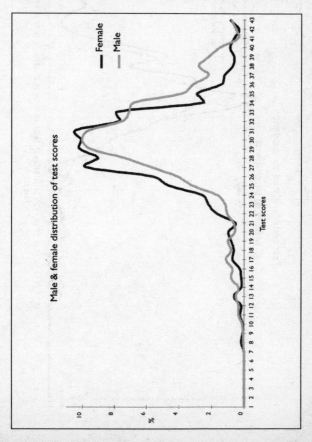

Male & female distribution of test scores

The next two charts illustrate the test results of those who claimed to have had no accidents in the last three years against those who admitted to an accident in the last three years. The first (below)

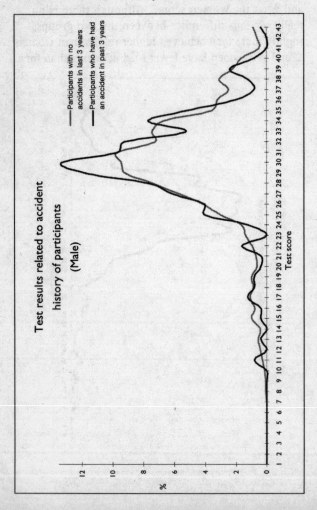

Test results related to accident
history of participants
(Male)

—— Participants with no accidents in last 3 years

—— Participants who have had an accident in past 3 years

Test score

shows men; the second (below), women. Peaks and troughs in the distribution of scores appear to be far more pronounced for both men and women if they have had an accident in the past three years.

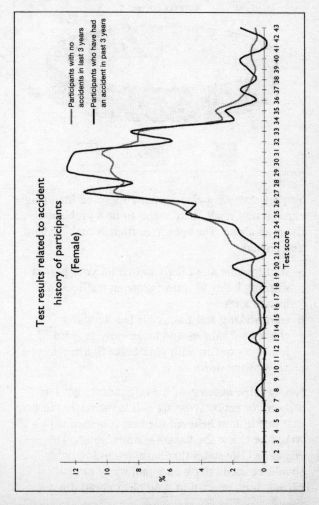

Test results related to accident history of participants
(Female)

—— Participants with no accidents in last 3 years

—— Participants who have had an accident in past 3 years

Test score

The following four charts show a breakdown of how people responded to four particular questions.

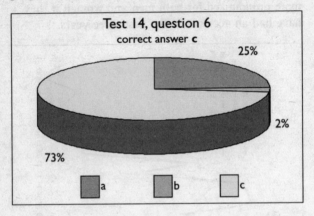

Test 14, question 6
correct answer **c**

25%

2%

73%

a   b   c

You are travelling along a national speed limit single carriageway road. There seems to be a problem on the road ahead. The vehicle in front is braking hard. You should

a start braking and briefly switch on your hazard warning lights to warn following traffic of a hazard ahead

b start braking and flash your headlights

c check your mirrors and brake early to warn following traffic, with your brake lights, that you are slowing down

Nearly three-quarters of the respondents got this answer correct by selecting **c**. It is interesting to note that one in four believed the best course of action would be to use the hazard warning lights. The *Highway Code* states that hazard warning lights should be used briefly on a motorway or dual carriageway, to warn of a problem ahead. On a motorway or dual carriageway, if you see the vehicle in front of you braking, you would usually check your mirrors to see if it is safe to change lanes. Hazard warning lights let you know that you should think twice about changing lanes. On a single carriageway, it is not necessary to use your hazard warning lights because your brake lights give sufficient warning of the fact that you are slowing down.

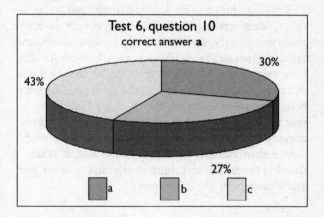

Test 6, question 10
correct answer **a**

30%

43%

27%

a   b   c

You are moving away on a very steep downhill gradient. What should you do?

a Select second gear, firmly brake, release the handbrake and move off when it is safe.
b Select first gear, bring the clutch to the biting point and move off when it is safe.
c Select first gear, firmly brake, release the handbrake and move off when it is safe.

This question confused people. Just under one third got it correct, whilst almost one in two people thought you should move away in first gear. More than one in four thought you should do an uphill start on a downhill gradient.

In the end, the decision to move away in first or second gear on a downhill gradient is subjective and depends on how steep you judge the gradient to be. You have to be there. So, it is understandable that 43% might choose to move away in first gear because their experience of a 'very steep gradient' is that it is not so steep that it warrants second gear.

Similarly, judgements about 'narrow roads', 'fast lanes', 'slow-moving traffic' are subjective. In practice, these non-specific descriptions affect people's decision-making processes in different ways, which means that how you choose to drive in a particular situation will not necessarily be the same as the driver in front or behind you. For example, the *Highway Code* states that you may overtake on the left in queues of slow-moving traffic, where traffic on the right is moving slower than you are. On a busy motorway, at what speed is the traffic travelling slowly and how do you know when you are in a queue?

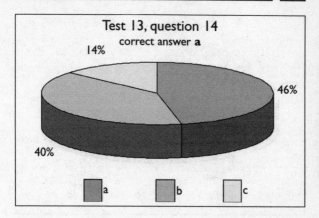

Test 13, question 14
correct answer **a**

14%

46%

40%

a   b   c

You are about to overtake a vehicle that is moving slower than you are. Which sequence of actions would be most likely to keep the manoeuvre safe?

a Mirrors – Position – Speed – Look – Mirrors – Signal – Manoeuvre
b Mirrors – Signal – Manoeuvre
c Mirrors – Signal – Position – Speed – Look.

Nearly half of the respondents in the sample got this question correct but 2 out of 5 chose MSM as their preferred sequence of actions when overtaking. Mirrors – Signal – Manoeuvre is fine; however, it means the decision to go has already been made and if it is the only sequence of actions that is used before actually pulling out to overtake, the decision may not have been safely thought through.

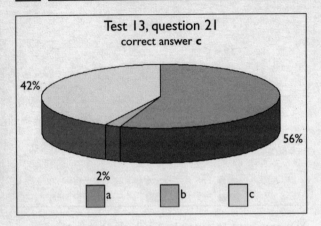

Test 13, question 21
correct answer **c**

42%

56%

2%

a   b   c

You are driving along a road in town. There is traffic following you. Some distance ahead is a parked car with a junction off to the right opposite it. There is no oncoming traffic and plenty of room for you to pass the parked car. Would you give a right-hand signal before moving out?

a Yes. A signal informs other road users of your intentions

b No. If you pull out early enough, your position acts as a signal informing other road users of your intentions

c No. There is a side road to the right and your signal might mislead other road users.

Why would 58% of the respondents in the sample get this question wrong? Is it conceivable that, in practice, 56% of them would signal their intentions to pass a parked car when there is a junction on the right just opposite? Would they not consider that a following driver might assume they are turning off to the right? Possibly the question was misread and

a was the preferred choice simply because it was a familiar sentence.

You have just read how the sample of people on the Internet responded to four of the questions in the IQ test and seen how much their opinions varied. Many of the responses to the other 39 questions showed similar degrees of variance. The average score for the test on the Internet was 31 out of 43, which is 72%.

The response to the IQ test on the Internet was staggering. No one could have predicted that so many people would have taken the time to answer all the questions. The fact that 2,760 did respond indicates the degree to which driving is involved in people's lives.

Hopefully, you have enjoyed this section and found it interesting and informative. It will perhaps have given you food for thought about how you drive and how to develop safer driving, irrespective of gender, age or driving experience.

FUN QUESTIONS

SECTION FOUR
TEST 1

1 In which decade did the UK see its first double-decker coaches?

_____

2 The qualifying examination to become a DSA Approved Driving instructor is in three sections:
The written test
The eyesight and driving technique test
The instructional ability test
What are each of these three tests called?

_____

_____

_____

3 When was the RAC first formed?

_____

4 The Driving Standards Agency maintains a national list of approved driving instructor training establishments. What is the name of the list?

_____

5 In which year did it first become compulsory for under 14s to wear rear seat belts?

_____

6 Complete this sentence: In driving instruction the pupil's level of ability will dictate the instructor's level of

_____

7 Compulsory M.O.T. testing was first introduced into the UK in which year?

_____

8 What does DB stand for in Aston Martin DB5?

_____

9 In which year did the first UK 70 mph limit get introduced?

_____

10 Which make of car did Michael Caine drive in *The Italian Job*?

_____

11 The *Highway Code* was first introduced in which year?

_____

12 Which make of car did Terry in *Minder* drive?

_____

13 What was Henry Ford's first designed car named?

_____

14 Until 1965, driving was done on the left-hand side on roads in Sweden. At what time of the day was the conversion to the right-hand side of the road made?

_____

15 The first traffic wardens appeared on UK streets in which year?

_____

16 The surface speed record on the moon was set in a lunar rover. What was the speed?

_____

17 What and where was the first motorway service station to open in Britain?

_____

_____

18 Match the town with its appropriate coastline. Score half a point for each correct answer.

1 Isle of Grain	a North East		
2 Redcar	b East East South		
3 St. David's	c West West South		
4 Ellesmere Port	d West West North		
5 Lowestoft	e South South West		
6 Polperro	f East		

19 Drivers and front seat passengers were required by law to wear seat belts in the UK in which year?

_____

20 What do Americans call the boot of the car?

_____

21 In which year did the first vehicular traffic use the Channel tunnel?

_____

22 In which year was the last Triumph TR6 made and the Triumph TR7 launched?

_____

23 Passenger trams were a means of transport within cities throughout the world during the late 19th century until the mid 20th century. Trams first returned to the UK in which city and in which year?

_____

24 What was the name of Henry Ford's son?

_____

25 Which year saw a change in legislation that meant anyone giving paid tuition to car drivers had to qualify as an Approved Driving Instructor and enter on to the register of Approved Driving Instructors?

_____

26 When an airbag deploys, what is the name of the gas produced?

_____

27 The first motor insurance policy was 'Third Party'. In which year did the Road Traffic Act make it compulsory to hold this type of insurance cover?

_____

28 Who founded the 'Motor' City of Detroit in the 17th century?

_____

29 What was the first car offered for sale and in which year?

_____

30 In which year did engineer Frederick Royce and car dealer Charles Rolls introduce their first car?

_____

31 In which year did traffic wardens first start issuing parking tickets?

_____

32 How long does an airbag take to inflate after a crash?

_____

33 Which two TV chefs used to ride a motorcycle and sidecar during the opening credits of their show?

_____

34 Match the songs to the artists:

1 Tom Robinson Band   **a** *Autobahn*

2 Kraftwerk   **b** *Cars*

3 Gary Numan   **c** *2-4-6-8 Motorway*

35 Pascal Norris used his Reliant Rialto as a hearse, taking his father's body to the crematorium in Carlisle. Which seat did he have to remove to get the coffin in?

_____

36 Match the songs to the artists:

1 Cyndi Lauper   **a** *I drove all night*

2 Wilson Pickett   **b** *Leader of the pack*

3 The Shangri-las   **c** *Mustang Sally*

37 What was the original 'Trotters Independent Traders Co' van from the TV comedy *Only Fools and Horses*?

_____

38 Name the film which contains a very famous car chase scene and stars Steve McQueen, Robert Vaughan, Jacqueline Bisset, Robert Duvall.

_____

39 What was the name of the famous champion-racing driver from the 1970s comic book *Tiger*?

_____

40 Name the film in which Matthew Broderick borrows his dad's old Ferrari.

_____

SECTION FOUR
TEST 2

1 The first breathalyser was introduced into the UK in which year?

_____

2 In order to qualify as a driving instructor you may have as many attempts as required to pass the written test. How many attempts are you allowed to pass the driving test and the instructional ability test?

_____

3 When was BSM first formed?

_____

4 On the driving technique test, the second part of the three-part qualifying examination to become an ADI, what is the maximum number of driver errors a candidate can make and still pass?

_____

5 In which year did the Dartford crossing open?

_____

6 A system of safe driving was developed in the United States in 1957 and subsequently imported to Britain by BSM. It comprises the following elements: Look well ahead, Move your eyes, Spot the problems, Keep space, Be seen. What is the name given to this system?

_____

7 Hemel Hempstead, in Hertfordshire, boasts a 'Magic Roundabout'. In which year was it opened?

8 What was the name of the 'Lovebug'?

9 Belisha beacons were introduced into the UK in which year?

10 Which car did James Bond drive in which film?

1 *The Man with the Golden Gun*	**a** Bentley	
2 *Goldfinger*	**b** AMC Hornet	
3 *From Russia with Love*	**c** Aston Martin DB5	

11 The first M.O.T. test was conducted in the UK in February 1961. The test was initially conducted on what age of vehicle?

12 Which make of car were Thelma and Louise driving in the film of the same name?

13 Double white lines, restricting overtaking, were first introduced into the UK in which year?

14 Figueroa Street in Los Angeles is the longest street in the world. How many miles does it cover?

_____

15 The Transport Research Institute carried out trials on speed ramps in the UK during the early 1970s. In which year did the first 'Road Hump' regulations commence?

_____

16 What is the ratio of cars to people in Los Angeles?

_____

17 The first Grand Prix was staged in 1901. What was the average speed recorded?

_____

18 Where is the only place in Britain where the National Speed limit sign still retains its original meaning of 'de-restriction'?

_____

19 The first vehicle-activated traffic lights were introduced into the UK in which year?

_____

20 In which year did production of the Morris Minor cease?

_____

21 In which year did zebra crossings come into use on British roads?

_____

22 Who said, 'The horse is here to stay, but the automobile is only a novelty, a fad'?

_____

23 Fill in the blank space. The first family hatchback to be produced was the

_____

24 In which year was the Ford Escort the UK's best seller?

_____

25 The first breakdown lorry was introduced into the UK in Newcastle-on-Tyne in which year?

_____

26 If your car was parked with the engine switched off and another car bumped into it, would the airbag be deployed?

_____

27 In which city of the UK did vehicle clamping first start, by whom was it implemented and in which year?

_____

28 In which year were Daewoo cars launched and sold direct to the public?

_____

29 What was the name of the first man to pass a British driving test?

_____

30 Name the plumbing inventor and manufacturer who built his first car in 1900.

_____

31 In which year was the first B & E test introduced?

_____

32 Name the mechanic, race car driver then race car team owner whose cars dominated racing for many years after the Second World War.

_____

33 The Isetta three-wheeled bubble car was conceived by Renzo Rivolta. What was his company ISO SPA famous in Italy for making?

_____

34 An airbag moves up to what speed within a second when triggered?

_____

35 The first motorised tricycle was reputedly made in Germany in 1885. Who made it?

_____

36 How many trips from an American home involve the use of a car? And how many trips from a British home involve the use of a car?

_____

37 Gordon McMinnies won the first ever 'Cycle Car Grand Prix' held at Amiens in France in 1913. He covered 162.9 miles. How long did it take him?

  a 5 hours, 32 minutes, 12 seconds.
  b 4 hours, 17 minutes, 57 seconds.
  c 3 hours, 53 minutes, 09 seconds.

38 Match the songs to the artists:

  1 Adam and   **a** *Drive*
     the Ants   **b** *Driving in my*
  2 REM   *car*
  3 Madness   **c** *Cartrouble*

39 The first recorded design for a self-propelled vehicle was by Guido da Vigevano. Power was provided by wind-driven sails. When was this?

_____

40 Match the songs to the artists:

  1 Michael Jackson **a** *Drive my car*
  2 Depeche Mode   **b** *Behind the wheel*
  3 Beatles   **c** *Speed demon*

1 When was the first UK driving test taken?

_____

2 The register of Approved Driving Instructors (car) was set up to operate in the interests of road safety. Approximately how many ADIs are on the register now?

_____

3 Where was the first UK motorway built and in which year?

_____

4 What are the three core competencies that form the basis of good driving instruction?

_____

_____

_____

5 The second Severn bridge was opened in which year?

_____

6 Which is the only road in London to have a different speed limit in each direction?

_____

7 The first car-towed caravan was made by whom and in which year?

_____

8 What was the number plate of the Saint's car in the TV series *The Saint*?

_____

9 The first Theory Test was introduced into the UK in which year?

_____

10 What did Basil Fawlty drive in *Fawlty Towers*?

_____

11 In which year did Karl Benz produce the world's first petrol-driven motor vehicle?

_____

12 Which make of car does Morse drive?

_____

13 Where were the first parking meters found in the UK?

_____

14 If you could drive to the sun, how many years would it take to get there? Imagine you are driving at a speed of 55 miles per hour.

_____

15 Where was the first petrol pump found in the UK and in which year?

_____

16 How wide is St John's Lane, a street in Rome?

_____

17 Speed cameras were first introduced on to UK roads in which year and where?

_____

18 What is 'Volvo' Latin for?

_____

19 Amphicars were built in Berlin between 1962 and 1967. What engines did they use in them?

_____

20 Who said, 'In less than 25 years the motorcar will be obsolete, because the aeroplane will run along the ground as well.'?

_____

21 In which year did the M25 open?

_____

22 In which year did BMW acquire Rover?

_____

23 Rear view mirrors became compulsory in which year?

_____

24 At around what speed does an airbag inflate?

_____

25 The first voluntary register for Approved Driving Instructors was introduced in which year?

_____

26 What do the following famous people have in common: Marc Bolan, James Dean, Jayne Mansfield?

_____

27 The 30 mph urban speed limit was first introduced on to UK roads in which year?

_____

28 What do the letters MG, found on the octagonal badge on certain sports cars, stand for?

_____

29 In which year did the first roundabout open in the UK and where?

_____

30 When rallying, what must be displayed on your helmet or overalls?

_____

31 In which year was the first Ministry of Transport established?

_____

32 Match the songs to the artists:

1 Prince	a *Route 66*
2 Bruce Springsteen	b *Little red corvette*
3 Chuck Berry	c *Pink Cadillac*

33 Computerised warning signs on British motorways were first introduced in which year?

_____

34 Who owns BSM and RAC?

_____

35 What was the registration number of Wallace and Gromit's motorcycle and sidecar in *A Close Shave*?

_____

36 Name the film based on a Stephen King novel about a possessed car.

_____

37 Which three-wheeler was originally designed as a form of non-motorised invalid carriage for ex servicemen but later became the basis for a successful motorised three-wheeler?

_____

38 Name the agency which licenses all BSM driving instructors.

_____

39 In which James Bond film is the principal car a Toyota 2000GT?

_____

40 What is the top speed of the Crawler, the transporter that takes the US space shuttle to its launch pad?

_____

ANSWERS

1 During the 1950s
2 Part One, Part Two, Part Three.
3 1897
4 ORDIT (Official Register of Driving Instructor Trainers)
5 1989
6 Instruction
7 1960
8 David Brown
9 1967
10 Mini Cooper
11 1931
12 Ford Capri 2.0s
13 Model T Ford
14 5pm. All traffic stopped as people switched sides. This time and day were chosen to prevent accidents where drivers might have woken up in the morning and forgotten that 'this' was the day of the changeover.
15 1960
16 10.56 miles per hour
17 M1 – between junctions 14 and 15, Newport Pagnell, 1959
18 1. b; 2. a; 3. c; 4. d; 5. f; 6. e

Give yourself half a point for each correct pairing (total points available are three).
19 1983
20 The trunk
21 1994
22 1976
23 1992, Manchester
24 Edsell
25 1970
26 Nitrogen. This is harmless and makes up 80% of the air we breathe.
27 1930
28 Antoine Cadillac
29 The Benz, 1887
30 1904
31 1960
32 40 milliseconds
33 Clarissa Dickson-Wright & Jennifer Patterson
34 1. c; 2. a; 3. b
Give yourself one point for each correct pairing.
35 The front passenger seat.
36 1. a; 2. c; 3. b
Give yourself one point for each correct pairing.

37 A Reliant Regal Supervan III.

38 *Bullit*

39 Skid Solo

40 *Ferris Bueller's Day Off*

SECTION FOUR	TEST 2

1 1967

2 Three each

3 1910

4 Six driver errors

5 1991

6 The Five Habits. The Smith-Cummings-Sherman visual search system was devised in the United States in 1957. Three researchers, Harold A. Smith, John J. Cummings and Reuel A. Sherman, collaborated on a project to investigate how accident-free drivers stay safe. Smith worked for the Ford Motor Company in its fleet division, Cummings was an accident investigator and Sherman was an ophthalmic expert. From the research a core set of principles was devised in the form of Five Good Driving Habits.

7 1973

8 Herbie

9 1934

10 1. b; 2. c; 3. a

Give yourself one point for each correct answer.

11 10 years or older.

12 Ford Thunderbird

13 1957

14 30 miles

15 1983

16 2:1

17 46 mph

18 Isle of Man

19 1932

20 1970

21 1951

22 Bank President, advising against investment in Ford, 1903. Sourced from the *Daily Mail*, 24.3.00

23 Renault 16

24 1992

25 1902

26 No. The airbag sensors will not trigger when the ignition is switched off.

27 London (Camden, Kensington, Chelsea, Westminster, City of London); Metropolitian Police; 1986

28 1995

29 Mr Beane

30 David Buick

31 1997

32 Enzo Ferrari

33 Fridges

34 4500 mph

35 Karl Benz

36 94% and 60% respectively.

37 The correct answer is **c**.

38 1. c; 2. a; 3. b
Give yourself one point for each correct answer.

39 1335

40 1. c; 2. b; 3. a
Give yourself one point for each correct answer.

SECTION FOUR	TEST 3

1 1935

2 33,000 (*The Official Guide for Driving Instructors*, 1998)

3 Preston by-pass (M6), 1958

4 Fault identification
Fault analysis
Remedial action

5 1996

6 Park Lane in central London.

7 1919, Eccles Motor Transport.

8 ST1

9 1996

10 Austin 1300

11 1885

12 Jaguar Mk II

13 Grosvenor Square, London.

14 193 years

15 1913, Shrewsbury

16 19 inches

17 West London, 1991

18 I roll

19 Triumph Herald
Sir Philip Gibbs, science journalist, 1928.

Sourced from the *Daily Mail*, 24.3.00.

21 1986

22 1994

23 1932

24 Around 200 mph

25 1964

26 They were all killed in car accidents.

27 1935

28 Morris Garages. Morris Garages was the first Oxford distributor for Morris cars.

29 1910, Letchworth, Hertfordshire.

30 Your blood group

31 1919

32 1. b; 2. c; 3. a
Give yourself one point for each correct answer.

33 1968

34 Lex

35 WAL 1

36 *Christine*

37 The Messerschmitt

38 The Driving Standards Agency.

39 *You Only Live Twice*

40 2 miles per hour